OR Purchase

O'
hos

ONE WEEK LOAN

CONTENTS

APPENDICES

INTRODUCTION

I remember sitting in an austere, cold classroom in RAF Henlow, during my officer training in 1973, watching the instructor drawing three overlapping circles on the blackboard (no PowerPoint then!) and writing the words *task, team* and *individual* in them. How strange it is for me now, some 37 years later, to be writing a book which is based upon the same leadership theory I was being introduced to back then.

The theory is called Action Centred Leadership (ACL) and it has certainly endured the passage of time. Indeed, it was created by a gentleman called John Adair in his first book entitled *Training for Leadership* in 1968 and has been embraced and applied by industry, commerce, and the military since then. It also forms the basis of the training that my company delivers to supervisors and junior managers from the hospitality, leisure, travel and tourism (HLTT) industry because I believe that it offers a practical approach to leadership ideally suited to the practical people who lead teams in my industry. Appendix A gives more details of John Adair and his work.

I have worked in hospitality all my working life: after serving 16 years in the Royal Air Force as a catering officer, I ran my own restaurant as chef-proprietor; managed the catering, conference and residential services at a UK university; and, for the past 12 years, have run my own company, Hospitality Leadership Ltd, that seeks to enhance standards of leadership, at all levels, through a range of developmental services.

There is so much written about leadership that you may ask what benefit there could be from yet another book, like this one. Apparently, if you set out to read every book on the subject from those available through Amazon you would be claiming your old age pension long before you got even halfway through them. So what is so special about this one? I believe that its uniqueness stems from the fact that it is written for a specific industry, by a person who has a deep understanding of both the industry itself, and those who work in it. The book does not include or propose in-depth, academic approaches to leadership – because I do not believe that its application requires the knowledge of detailed or complex theories. In its simplest form, as Sir John Harvey-Jones described it:

"Leadership is about getting extraordinary performance out of ordinary people."

It is not rocket science. We all know what inspires us to greater effort so why should it be difficult to apply those principles to those we, ourselves, lead. There are so many well-known phrases that, actually, infer leadership principles, such as:

'Actions speak louder than words'

'Never ask anyone to do something you wouldn't do yourself'

'Treat people how you would like to be treated yourself'

If I was to give one simple piece of advice to someone taking up the mantle of leadership in my, or indeed any, industry – my Pearl of Wisdom – it would be an amended version of the last phrase quoted above, namely:

'Lead people how you would like to be led'

That is not to say that everyone has the same motivational stimuli, because they don't. We all respond differently; and a key requirement for a leader is to identify how best to inspire each individual member of his or her team. My point is that all of us do know how <u>we</u> 'would like to be led'. Hence, in that knowledge, my advice to all leaders is to recognise that fact and apply it to their team members by working hard to understand what will best motivate each one of them to reach their potential. Some may be motivated by financial reward (although fewer than you may imagine); some will respond best to development opportunities; others to being offered additional responsibilities; most, if not all, to praise and recognition.

If, as I propose, effective leadership is based upon principles that most people can understand, why is it that so many people holding leadership positions apparently seem unable, or unwilling, to apply them? I am sure that many readers of this book have had personal experiences of poor management that supports this supposition as does, I am afraid, research undertaken within our industry.

The first stage of the Sector Skills Agreement conducted by People1st, the Sector Skills Council for the HLTT industry, involved consultation with around 5,000 industry employers and found that:

- Graduates entering the sector at junior management level lacked practical experience.

- Functionally good staff at craft skills level were given managerial posts without appropriate training; some of whom lack the necessary management qualities.

- Young people, perhaps in their mid-twenties, were being promoted to managerial positions without the necessary experience to deal with difficult people-management situations.

There is no doubt that the hospitality industry offers marvellous career development opportunities for a young person who is prepared to work hard and grasp those that are offered. Yet promotion must be supported by training and development in management and leadership skills. As one respondent in People1st's consultation observed: *"Many managers move up through promotions, which is common in this industry. They need team leadership skills, motivational skills."*

The research further identified that:

- Less than 50 per cent of managers in the sector have received any formal management training.

- One third of employers do not train their staff and ...

- Twenty-five per cent say that nothing will get them to train them!

- The current staff turnover figure in the HLTT industry is at least thirty per cent; with that within hospitality possibly double that.

- Managers' actions and attitudes greatly impact on staff turnover, which cost the sector at least £885m every year.

What a sad reflection on standards of leadership within some HLTT companies and organisations. It can only be that there are too many people holding leadership positions, at all levels, who are simply poor leaders. I call them 'badge holders': they have the badge of leadership – perhaps on their office door that says 'Chief Executive'; or on their desk that says 'General Manager'; or on their whites proclaiming them to be the 'Head Chef' – but that does not mean they are good leaders.

I hope that this book will provide both guidance and inspiration for those currently holding a leadership position, at any level, within the HLTT industry, as well as those aspiring to do so. The first part of the book explores the subject of leadership from a number of angles; including some thoughts about what leadership actually is and how previous research has contributed to that understanding; how ACL can be applied within a hospitality operation; and how organisations can develop their leaders to meet the challenge of the twenty-first century.

However, so many of us have been inspired by great people we have known or worked with in the past. In a working environment we learn many of our leadership lessons from past managers, good or bad; hence the second part of the book includes the stories of leadership champions from our own industry. From a McDonald's restaurant manager who has a deep understanding of the roles and responsibilities of a team leader, to a director of a contract catering company who has successfully made the transition from operational to strategic leadership, we can learn so many leadership lessons to take back to our own roles.

This book is for those who *'aspire to inspire'*.

Alan Cutler FIH FCMI
Hospitality Leadership Ltd

1.1 WHAT IS LEADERSHIP?

I enjoy quotations as they provide an endless source of wit and wisdom and inspiration. Indeed, my first book, entitled *'Leadership Quote/Unquote'*, used over 200 quotations to reinforce the leadership messages contained within it. When faced with a challenge you can be sure that someone else has faced it before you and made some profound comment on the subject. One such challenge could be to define leadership and you will not be surprised to learn that there are plenty of definitions contained in the 25,000, or so, works that have been written on the subject. In 1974 the American psychologist, Ralph Stogdill, sought to consolidate a list and identified 160 different definitions, grouped into ten different categories.

No doubt those of us who are interested in the subject have our own favourites. Certainly there are plenty to choose from; from the concise:

> *"Leadership is action, not position"*

Donald H McGannon

through the academic:

> *"Leadership is the influential increment over and above the mechanical compliance with the routine directives of the organisation"*

Katz and Kahn

and the poetic:

> *"The shepherd always tries to persuade the sheep that their interests and his own are the same"*

Henri B Stendhal

to the rather chilling:

> *"The art of leadership consists of consolidating the attention of the people against a simple adversary and taking care that nothing will split up that attention"*

Adolf Hitler

and the descriptive:

> *"If people are coming to work excited; if they are making mistakes freely and fearlessly; if they are having fun; if they are concentrating on doing things, rather than preparing reports and going to meetings - then somewhere you have leaders"*

Robert Townsend

One thing is for certain: the subject of leadership is guaranteed to get people talking. As John Adair, himself, says:

"Leadership is one of the most mysterious and fascinating subjects in the world"

I have lost count of the number of times in a social environment, after having asked what I do for a living, people become engaged and start posing some old leadership chestnuts, such as: are leaders born or made; is there a difference between leadership and management; do leaders need charisma? People, indeed, do find the subject both mysterious and fascinating and are usually all too keen to become engaged in a discussion on some aspect of it. Later in this chapter I will attempt to address and de-mystify some of the perennial questions. However, before then we need to understand where leaders operate in an organisation.

Levels of Leadership

In my past reading into, and discussions about, the subject of leadership I have come to the conclusion that many people consider that leaders sit only at the very top of an organisation; setting its strategic direction and taking all the important decisions. Yet all organisations of any size have people working in different departments, with different roles and responsibilities who report to different managers. Whilst the chief executive may be the most senior decision maker, others throughout the organisation have tasks to complete – which they invariably do through the efforts of teams of people for whom they are responsible. From the

Chairman of the Board to the Supervisor who has a team of customer-facing staff, the leadership function is required at every level. That said, if we are to consider the application of leadership throughout an organisation, we need to simplify the structure into various levels of leadership. I propose three:

Team Leaders – those who have responsibility for perhaps up to 20 people employed in a single working area. In the hospitality industry, these could be head receptionists, restaurant managers, or school kitchen supervisors.

Operational Leaders – middle managers to whom a number of team leaders report: perhaps a food and beverage manager, or someone responsible for a medium-sized unit.

Strategic Leader – those who have responsibility for shaping the strategic direction of an organisation, or are owners of their own business.

Whilst some aspects of leadership will be common to all three levels, we shall see that the functions that they have to undertake get more complex and numerous the higher the level. Having said that, we must not minimise the importance of the team leader to the success of the organisation as a whole. Indeed, I would propose that it is the team leader upon whom its success primarily depends. It is the front-line staff, led by their team leaders, who are in a position to make the customer satisfied or dissatisfied; return or never set foot in the restaurant again. We all measure an organisation by the attitude and professionalism provided by those who serve us – not by the chief executive. Highly motivated staff, led by inspirational team leaders, will create loyal customers who act as ambassadors for, and form the foundation of, any successful company. Conversely, demotivated, disinterested staff simply turn customers away. It is team leaders who, through their leadership or lack of it, create ambassadors or assassins for their organisations. Yet, who can inspire team leaders – operational leaders, of course. And so it happens through the leadership levels, reinforcing the point that inspirational leadership is required throughout the organisation.

Are Leaders Born or Made?

Perhaps the oldest leadership chestnut: to what extent does inherent personality, pre-determined at birth, form the foundation of great leadership? Or can the necessary building blocks be learnt and developed during one's life, especially in the formative years? Opinion is split: some people believe that great leaders are born with that special something that makes them rise, inevitably, up the leadership ladder; whilst others believe that leadership skills can be learnt by anyone. Here's how the polarised arguments go:

Leaders are born. This belief, applied to the 'Great Man' theory of leadership, assumes leadership is an innate gift that cannot be taught or learnt. Certain people are born with in-bred characteristics and abilities that make it inevitable that they will assume the mantle of leadership. They have certain natural strengths that lend themselves to leadership, for example a willingness and desire to influence others; a determination to succeed; a thirst for perfection; and being sociable, warm and affectionate. Certainly, one might consider that the former US President Bill Clinton and the current incumbent Barack Obama portray many of those strengths: having a charismatic presence and a desire to take charge of a situation.

Yet, whilst no doctor delivering a baby would hold it up proudly and announce to the parents *"It's a leader"*, proponents of the 'leaders are born' theory believe that leadership qualities are present, if not identifiable and developed, at birth. Furthermore, these characteristics display themselves early in life: it is apparent watching primary school children in the playground that some follow and some lead. Yet such children do not at that stage exist in hierarchical, organisational structures that will certainly influence their later life. The reason they willingly follow certain of their peers is that the latter children are already displaying a leader's persona they were born with.

<u>Leaders are made</u>. The counter philosophy is that anyone, if he or she is motivated enough, can be a successful leader, as leadership skills can be acquired through learning, training and application. Indeed, most MBA courses include formal training on the requirements of leadership in business. That said, most people who contend that leaders are made believe that more can be learnt through experience than by attending courses. Indeed, in 2002, Warren Bennis and Robert Thomas interviewed 40 top leaders from business and the public sector to identify how they had learnt to be a leader. All of them attributed their leadership abilities to having encountered, and successfully overcome, great challenges in their lives – whilst none mentioned formal leadership development programmes run by organisations.

Everybody has leadership potential, it is believed, although modesty or lack of experience can create self-doubt. However, opportunities for leadership occur every day so even the most reluctant people occasionally find themselves having to take charge of a situation or a group of people. Each situation is different and, whilst those of a high profile nature attract more attention, even routine events offer the potential to develop leadership skills.

<u>A compromise theory</u>? Perhaps the answer lies between the two previous positions, taking aspects of both. Surely we are all born with different innate characteristics, some of which are amply apparent within the first few weeks of life – ask any new parent! Could not some of these characteristics make us more, or less, likely to support the future development of leadership skills?

That said, we cannot ignore the influences that outside agencies – family, schooling, friends, mentors, training (formal or informal) – can have on our development. Nobody is saying that a young person from a dysfunctional family, growing up on a crime-ridden, inner-city housing estate could never develop outstanding leadership skills. There are many examples of leaders who have emerged from the most unlikely, challenging backgrounds. Colin Powell, for example, the son of Jamaican immigrants, joined the US Army shortly after it accepted black recruits and served in the southern states of America, which, at the time, were far from being racially integrated. Yet he rose to be a four-star general and, later, Secretary of State.

Whilst some great leaders have, indeed, come from extremely deprived backgrounds, any natural leadership skills may be more likely to emerge from within a supportive environment. Here, the young person has many positive role models to learn from and a multitude of opportunities to develop any leadership potential he or she has. The more encouragement exists, the more likely that leaders will emerge. So the compromise theory is that both inherited and learnt factors play a part. All people are born with characteristics that make them more, or less, likely to develop leadership skills, but the extent to which the in-born predisposition develops its potential is heavily influenced by the opportunities that present themselves and the learning, formal or experiential, that occurs.

But what does academic research suggest in terms of the part that genetics play?

In 2005, Richard Arvey, Professor of Human Resources and Industrial Relations at the University of Minnesota, conducted a study of 325 pairs of identical and fraternal male twins who were born between 1961 and 1964 and were raised together. Previous studies of twins that were reared apart had proved that similarities in terms of personality, interests and attitudes were due to genes, rather than environmental influences: the environment makes them different, whilst their genes make them similar. As identical twins share one hundred per cent of their genes, with fraternal twins only about fifty per cent, Arvey's study aimed to quantify the contribution of genetics and environmental factors in leadership.

To do so, participants were asked a series of questions centred on the wish to influence others; a desire to be the centre of attention; the ability to persist when others give up;

and being comfortable in other people's company. The assumption was that, as those questions have a genetic component, if the respondents answered them positively they were probably 'genetically wired' for leadership. Professor Arvey then took an inventory of the leadership roles they had held throughout their lives, including as supervisors, directors, vice-presidents, or presidents. He explained, *"A great deal of personality is genetic-based. If your personality is such that you aspire to, and have held, these positions, then the roles also suggest a genetic link."*

What he found was that thirty per cent of leadership is based on genetics, whilst the remaining seventy per cent is dependent upon environmental factors. He concluded, *"While environmental influences determine many of our leadership behaviours and the roles we obtain, our genes still exert a sizeable influence over whether we will become leaders. Although thirty per cent may not seem like a high number, statistically it is strong. Leaders aren't just made!"*

It should be stated, however, that the study merely considered those who became leaders, and why. It did not take into consideration leadership effectiveness – some of the contributors could have been 'badge holders'! Nonetheless, the research does shed light on the 'are leaders born or made?' conundrum: suggesting that neither extreme position tells the complete story. It appears that leadership is both inherited and acquired. When examining the differences between individuals with regard to whether they took up leadership roles, over one quarter of the differences were explained by genetics. The remaining nearly three-quarters were accounted for by external influences such as training, job experiences and education, as well as other forms of environmental exposure.

What about Charisma?

I mentioned both Bill Clinton and Barrack Obama in the last section, as having certain natural leadership qualities that supported the 'leaders are born' argument. Many observers would describe them as being charismatic, along with other political leaders such as Mahatma Gandhi, Adolf Hitler, Winston Churchill and John F Kennedy; and those promoting their religious beliefs like Billy Graham, Martin Luther King and L Ron Hubbard.

But what makes a leader charismatic; what are the benefits and potential pitfalls of being so; and, most importantly, how essential is charisma to effective leadership?

Charismatic leaders have a firm belief that they can lead their followers by the power of their personal charm, without the necessity of external power or position. Either face-to-face, or by any indirect means, they seek to make those they meet feel like the most important person on the planet. In a group situation they 'work the room' as they move from person to person, giving each their full attention. They instinctively assess the mood and concerns of each individual and can even extend that ability when addressing larger audiences: adopting their words and actions to maximum effect in both scenarios. They are masters of body language – both using it personally and assessing it in others. Exceptional communication skills are, however, perhaps the most essential attribute of a charismatic leader – the ability to communicate on a very powerful emotional level.

The values that a charismatic leader promotes often define him or her: if they are well-intentioned and benevolent they can be transformational. If, however, they are self-serving or Machiavellian, history has proved that they can create powerful and destructive cults. As Patricia Sellers wrote in an article in the Fortune Magazine in 1996:

"Charisma is a tricky thing. Jack Kennedy oozed it – but so did Hitler and Charles Manson. Con artists, charlatans and megalomaniacs can make it their instrument as effectively as the best CEOs, entertainers and Presidents. Used wisely, it's a blessing; indulged, it can be a curse. Charismatic visionaries lead people ahead, and sometimes astray."

They believe in themselves so highly that they can easily be persuaded that they are infallible and, hence, will ignore advice and warnings as they lead their people into the abyss. Moreover, where the charismatic leader holds an influential position within a company or organisation, who will replace him or her? The incumbent may have been intolerant of challenges and, having relied very much on the power of personality, there may be no successors waiting in the wings. Relying so heavily on one leader's charisma, the danger is that the organisation is ill-prepared to move forward once that person leaves.

That said, whilst in post, charismatic leaders can create powerful allegiances within their group of people. They will often focus heavily on developing a group identity – creating a sense of elitism that separates it from other groups. The group identity will be inextricably linked at an emotional level to the leader, thus creating an unchallengeable position for itself. Hence, a charismatic leader whose objectives are well-founded and worthy can be a powerful force for good.

However, the reality is that few people have the necessary personal qualities, convictions and determination to become leaders of a charismatic nature. Moreover, developing charisma in oneself is difficult, if not impossible. It is fortunate, therefore, that being charismatic is not essential to be an effective, even an inspirational, leader. Many other characteristics and skills are involved in leading people and there is significant evidence to indicate that it is simply not necessary to have this elusive 'charisma' to lead people to achieve remarkable results.

In his book *Good to Great*, Jim Collins describes the results of five years researching American companies that made the leap from achieving good results to great results, and sustained them for at least 15 years. He also compared those to a control group of companies that either failed to make the leap or, if they did, failed to sustain it. The overall objective of the research was to discover what essential factors distinguished both groups. The good-to-great companies included well-known names such as Gillette, Kimberly-Clark and Wells Fargo. What Collins found was that the leaders of all these companies were, in fact, self-effacing individuals who did not seek the spotlight in any respect or at any time. They could, in no way, be described as charismatic; rather, modest and humble. That is not to say that they were found to have no ego or self-interest: they were, in fact, incredibly ambitious – but their ambition was, first and foremost, for their institution, rather than themselves. They channelled the needs of their ego away from themselves and into the larger goal of building a great company. They were truly inspirational leaders, motivating their people to create great companies – but not by having a charismatic personality.

Leadership and Management

This book is about hospitality leaders and leadership. But what about managers and management? Is there a difference between leadership and management? Are all good managers good leaders? Do we need both? In considering the differences, let us start with the origins of both words.

The word **manage** originates from the Latin for a hand. Hence, 'to manage' means to handle things, resources or, by extension, people – 'human resource management'.

Field Marshall Lord Slim used to tell the story that early in the 1900s the Indian Army produced an instructional pamphlet entitled *Mule Management*. Shortly after, not to be outdone, the War Office back in 'Blighty' produced a similar document that they called *Man Management* – hence, the term was born.

By contrast, the word **lead** derives from the Anglo-Saxon for a journey, a road, a way. Thus, leading is concerned with moving from one place to another; from one situation to another. Leading, therefore, involves change and it is in periods of great change that exceptional leaders emerge.

Management is therefore about handling resources; about maintaining and controlling the status quo; about ensuring that policies and procedures are executed to meet pre-determined targets and objectives. It is largely a mechanistic activity, being dealt with through balance sheets as far as finance is concerned; and through levels of authority in order to bring order to an organisation. Hard facts and measurable results are meat and drink to managers.

Leadership, on the other hand, is more people-focused, whilst still having agreed objectives in mind. It relates more to vision, inspiration and emotion, rather than control, discipline and logic.

One of the most often-quoted evaluations of the differences between leaders and managers is that of Warren Bennis, from his *Managing the Dream* article, published in 1990. It includes the following comparisons:

> The manager is a copy;
> The leader is an original.
>
> The manager focuses on systems and structures;
> The leader focuses of people.
>
> The manager relies on control;
> The leader inspires trust.
>
> The manager asks 'how' and 'when';
> The leader asks 'what' and 'why'.

> The manager has his eye on the bottom line;
> The leader has his eye on the horizon.
>
> The manager accepts the status quo;
> The leader challenges it.
>
> The manager does things right;
> The leader does the right thing.

Personally, I have a slight problem with Bennis's pairs of statements. Whilst it certainly graphically identifies the apparently different approaches of a manager and a leader; by the very use of those two words it suggests that people can be pigeonholed into being either a manager or a leader. Most people, like me, who have considered or researched the difference between leadership and management conclude that, for an organisation to exist and develop, both sound management and inspirational leadership are required.

In the research I conceived and led with Bournemouth University in 2006/7, The Hospitality Leadership Excellence Survey (an interim academic paper on which is included, along with additional updated findings, at Appendix B), I asked 25 hospitality leaders whether they felt that there was a difference between management and leadership. All agreed that there was, indeed, a difference: leadership was felt to be about creating a vision and inspiring others to follow it; whilst management was more concerned with process and controls – making sure the job got done. The respondents agreed that both good leaders and good managers were required to ensure the success of hospitality organisations and, hence, the industry as a whole.

In a typical hierarchical company the Board of Directors will, largely, provide the vision and direction to be adopted and translated into practical applications by the various tiers of management. Without the vision, the company will stagnate and wither; without sound working practices the company will not realise the potential required by the Board. That is not to say that creating a vision is the sole responsibility of leaders operating at a strategic level. Team leaders, for example, should also have a clear vision of what they want to achieve, through their team – to produce the best possible food; or to achieve very high customer satisfaction scores, perhaps.

The danger is, though, that an organisation becomes so process-driven that managers focus too much attention on targets that then stifle initiative and creativity – even measured risk taking, as was found by Jasminder Singh from Radisson Edwardian Hotels and described in Chapter 1.6. Bureaucracy takes hold and front-line operators are buried in endless red tape and rules. As Bennis has observed *"Failing organisations are usually over-managed and under-led"*. The potential hazard of this imbalance was further emphasised by some respondents in our industry-specific research, who commented:

> *"As an industry, we have great management. We are over-managed in places."*

"There are too many people in our industry who
think they are leaders, but actually are managers".

So, organisations, or indeed, teams of any size, need both visionary leadership <u>and</u> sound management. That is not to say, though, that good leaders necessarily make good managers, or the reverse – far from it. A financial manager or an engineer may continually meet, or exceed, targets, but may not have 'his eye on the horizon'. Conversely, a board member or an entrepreneur may have 'a long term perspective' but may lack the ability to make it happen.

Let me finish this section by offering an anonymous quotation that eloquently provides appropriate cautionary advice:

"We must not let the pearl of leadership be replaced by
the metal of management."

1.2 WHAT MAKES A GREAT LEADER

I know from experience in the training room that when I ask people who they think of as being great leaders the same names crop up time after time. They tend to be well known, high profile people, mainly male I am afraid, who have risen to prominence over the past few hundred years. They are often from a political or military background, although sometimes religious, sporting or community leaders are proposed. But, of course, few of us ever met Margaret Thatcher or Winston Churchill; and probably even fewer found ourselves in the presence of Nelson Mandela or Martin Luther King – and certainly none of us met Admiral Nelson or, hopefully, Adolf Hitler!

Yet these are the names we think of when we are asked to name great leaders, even though they never had a direct influence on our personal or working lives. We never worked with them or for them; their direct presence never inspired us to greater effort or to achieve more than we thought we were capable of. Surely, when we consider 'what makes a great leader' we should also look closer to home and consider those we have come into contact with at work; on the sports field; in our community; even in our family. What made them so influential? What differentiated them from other people holding a position of responsibility? Why would we follow them without question?

So, what does make a great leader? In his usual straightforward way John Adair suggests that the answer can be characterised by considering three separate aspects of leaders:

- What they are – the Qualities Approach
- What they know – the Situational Approach
- What they do – the Functional Approach

The Qualities Approach – what the leader IS

This is, perhaps, the traditional approach to defining effective leadership – to look at what personal qualities are required. A fundamental problem to this approach is quite simply: how can we specify what qualities are, or are not, required? The initial objective research into leadership as a concept began in the early years of the twentieth century when the commonly accepted view was that all leaders were born with certain personal qualities (the 'leaders are born' theory again) that were applicable for all fields of experience, at all times. The researchers began by collecting various lists of required leadership qualities from different sources and then analysing them to identify any commonality. What emerged was that there were, in fact, no common denominators. One celebrated study by Professor Bird in 1940 looked at 20 empirical studies on leadership and found that only five per cent of the qualities appeared in four or more studies: there was very little agreement as to which qualities define leadership. Everyone has their own thoughts and would draw up different lists; although there may well be some qualities that would appear on several of the lists.

John Adair, for instance, proposes and explains the following list of generic leadership qualities as:

Enthusiasm. The top of his list. It may be quiet and slow-burning enthusiasm, rather than passionate, but it is always there.

Integrity. This is the quality that engenders trust. It is the bedrock of good leadership; and leadership for good (not always the same thing!).

Toughness. Being demanding and not easily satisfied – and being prepared to make unpopular decisions, if required.

Fairness. In setting high standards, without compromise, a leader must be consistent and fair, whilst not asking from others what they do not require from themselves first.

Humanity. 'Cold fish' do not make good leaders. Leaders need to demonstrate an inner kindness or sympathy when the occasion calls for it.

Confidence. We all need a level of self-confidence if we are to put our talents to work and leaders are no different in this respect. Confidence should not, however, be confused with over-confidence.

<u>Humility</u>. A lack of arrogance, coupled with a willingness to admit one's mistakes. People respond to others who do not have an inflated opinion of themselves.

<u>Courage</u>. In non-military situations this is moral, rather than physical, courage: an ability to face up to and confront difficult situations.

<u>Resilience</u>. Leadership over the long haul requires a willingness and ability to bounce back after the inevitable setbacks.

Those are what John Adair believes are common, and universally necessary, qualities of effective leadership. However, when I asked the leaders I interviewed for The Hospitality Leadership Excellence Survey (Appendix B) what qualities were required, many suggested:

- Being visionary
- Having good communication skills, including listening
- Building relationships on a basis of trust, consistency and transparency
- Personal characteristics including humility and integrity
- Not being afraid of admitting one's mistakes
- Having a sense of humour

One can see there are definite parallels between the qualities contained in that list and those that John Adair proposes, but the lists are by no means the same. No two leadership thinkers propose the same required qualities: from today's thinking, right back to the third century BC when Xenophan, the professional soldier and writer, proposed temperance, justice, sagacity, amiability, presence of mind, tactfulness, humanity, sympathy, helpfulness, courage, magnanimity, generosity and considerateness.

Along with the difficulty in defining the necessary qualities, another problem with this approach is that it favours selection for leadership, rather than training and development. Indeed, it is only relatively recently that leadership was recognised as something that could actually be learnt. Even now, relatively few British universities include the subject within hospitality degree courses. That said, things are beginning to change and Leeds Metropolitan University have become the first to offer a degree in Hospitality Management and Leadership. In industry also, the more far-sighted companies such as Radisson Edwardian Hotels, Four Seasons Hotels and the Brookwood Partnership now recognise the crucial importance of effective leadership at all levels and are training their staff accordingly. The fact that People1st identified 'management and leadership' as one of the three industry skill shortages in its Skills Sector Agreement research, also indicates recognition of leadership as an individual skill to be developed.

If the traditional Qualities Approach favours the idea of selection rather than development, surely it runs the risk of ignoring the potential of talent that may need nurturing and encouragement, rather than being openly apparent at an early stage. A young manager once had written on his annual appraisal 'Smith is not a born leader yet'. If so, what can poor Smith, or indeed his organisation, do about it?

The Armed Forces offer us an interesting case study on leadership selection and development. Whereas centuries of belief was founded on 'The Great Man' theory of leadership,

"The Battle of Waterloo was won on the playing fields of Eton"

Sir William Fraser

views began to change around the beginning of the twentieth century. Field Marshal Montgomery was one of those who challenged the old assumptions when he wrote:

> Some will say that leaders are born, not made, and that you can't make a leader by teaching, or training. I don't agree with this entirely. While it is true that some men have within themselves the instincts and qualities of leadership in a much greater degree than others, and some men will never have the character to make leaders, I believe that leadership can be developed by training. By the training I had received from my superiors in peacetime, I gained confidence in my ability to deal with any situation likely to confront a young officer of my rank in war; this increased my morale and my powers of leading my platoon, and later my company.
>
> In other words, it is almost true to say that leaders are 'made' rather than born. Many men who are not natural leaders may have some small spark of the qualities which are needed; this spark must be looked for, and then developed and brought on by training.

I personally experienced the approach Montgomery proposed in his final sentence in my quest to become a catering officer in the Royal Air Force in 1973. Those who applied for a commission, and whose application form indicated a willingness to take up positions of responsibility in sporting or social environments, were invited to attend a two-day selection procedure at RAF Biggin Hill. There, we were put through a range of tests and practical exercises designed to assess our potential for leadership – *the small spark of the qualities which are needed* that Montgomery described. Those of us who passed through that process were subsequently put through 16 weeks officer training at RAF Henlow – which included a range of activities from classroom training to the arduous five day camp that we spent in the woods honing our leadership skills and sleeping under parachutes!

Fellow officer cadets and I were lucky at that time to have benefited from the new thinking on leadership selection and training that had been developed by John Adair when he worked at the Royal Military Academy, Sandhurst from 1961 to 1969. No doubt his thinking had been influenced by personal experience during his national service officer training when the only leadership training he received consisted of a sheet of paper with 32 qualities of leadership listed on it. He recalls that the officer cadet in the bed next to him took it very seriously. On Monday he practised 1-5 on the list; on Tuesday 6-10; and so on. The list for Thursday included 'a sense of humour', which he practised by reading the magazine Punch. At the end of the week he either felt he had mastered all the 32 qualities – which made him impossible to live with; or he thought he had none of them – which detracted from the confidence essential for leadership.

The officer training I experienced at RAF Henlow was not designed to <u>teach</u> leadership but to give young officers-to-be the opportunity to <u>learn</u> about it: to make discoveries as we explored our own practical experiences in the light of the founding principles of leadership we learnt in the classroom. The principle being that the best way to develop leadership skills is to practice them and find out what works best in different circumstances and environments. This is very much the approach upon which leadership training should be based, such as the *Inspirational Team Leadership* programme (Appendix C).

So what have we concluded about The Qualities Approach to leadership? There is no doubt that there are some generic qualities that leaders need to be able to apply in appropriate circumstances. The lists I included earlier in the chapter are indicative, but they are by no means exhaustive. I like to think of effective leaders having a tool box in which they hold a wide range of qualities that they can pull out and apply according to the situations they face, as well as according to the needs of the individuals and teams they are leading. A sense of humour can be a very effective tool at certain times, but would be most inappropriate at others!

"To the man who only has a hammer in the toolkit, every problem looks like a nail"

Abraham Maslow

The Qualities Approach does, therefore, offer a good deal of help to our understanding of leadership but, having certain drawbacks, it does not provide a single solution. Let us, therefore consider the second approach.

The Situational Approach – what the leader KNOWS

The Situational Approach emphasises the importance of knowledge to the effectiveness of a leader; whose authority is enhanced by the technical or professional know-how he or she possesses. The authority does not result from the leader's position in the organisation, or from his or her force of personality: it is confirmed by the depth of specialist knowledge held.

The leadership influence resulting from one's knowledge was first identified by Socrates in the fifth-century BC when he proposed *"In any situation, people will tend to follow or obey the man or woman who knows what to do, and how to do it."* The concept is well illustrated by imagining the survivors of a shipwreck who make their way to a tropical island. Whilst the ship's captain is one part of the group, his skills in terms of sailing and navigation will be of limited use in terms of the party's continual survival. The ship's carpenter would likely take the lead when shelters have to be built; the ship's cook would lead in the collection, preparation and cooking of the meals; whilst the soldier who was a passenger on board the ship would direct efforts to defend their interests if natives attacked them. In other words, leadership would pass around the group according to the demands of the situation, or task, they faced. It is the situation that determines who emerges as the leader and what style of leadership he or she adopts.

There is no doubt that possessing a degree of specialist knowledge can add to a leader's credibility in some followers' minds. Moreover, having 'the right man at the right time' can make the difference between brilliant success and abject failure. Perhaps the most dramatic and far-reaching example of this was Winston Churchill's leadership influence during the Second World War. His dogged determination, deep self-belief and ability to appeal to the hearts and minds of the British public were, surely, the most critical determining factors on the outcome of the war. He was certainly a 'man of his time', but once peace had been won the skills he applied during the conflict were less appropriate to the rebuilding of the country's society, economy and infrastructure, and he was quickly voted out of power.

Recognising the positive contribution that knowledge has to effective leadership is important to our understanding but, like the Qualities Approach, there are associated limitations: it does not offer the complete solution.

I guess that many of us remember people we have worked with who were very intelligent and who possessed exceptional specialist knowledge, but had little common sense and even less leadership ability. Indeed, they may have been given a managerial role merely on the basis of their academic qualifications. As a young boy I remember my father commenting on one such graduate who had joined his organisation with a first class degree, but third class practical ability. As I have grown up I have met a few myself! A brilliant salesman does not necessarily make a good sales manager. In our industry, a great chef may not make a great executive chef or kitchen manager.

Technical skill is especially important in the early stages of one's career but as we take on less specialist roles we need to be able to apply more general skills, such as leadership, communications and decision making. As we are promoted to supervisory roles we are increasingly faced with people-related challenges and, hence, must develop softer, less technical skills. Our job involves us spending less time and effort taking bookings or serving customers, with an increasing emphasis on leading those whose responsibility it is to do so. We are measured less on what we actually achieve ourselves and more on what our team achieves – a lesson many 'badge holders' have failed to grasp!

Another problem with the Situational Approach is that, in most working environments, leadership cannot easily be passed around the group. There must be someone in the group who has the vision and is accountable for setting priorities, making decisions and achieving results. Even on the desert island, whilst the carpenter is in charge of construction, the cook is responsible for feeding the crew, and even when the soldier is leading the charge against the natives, the ship's captain should remain in overall command. Whilst he may delegate the necessary task-related authority to his specialists, he still retains his supreme leadership position, including overall accountability for the success of each venture. Whilst he may not have the technical knowledge required of every situation, his general leadership skills will be required to ensure that every task is completed by the crew, either acting as individuals or in groups. How he does that will be the measure of the success of his leadership – which brings us on to the third approach to leadership.

The Functional Approach – what the leader DOES

This third approach to leadership focuses on what leaders <u>do</u>, as well as what they <u>are</u> and what they <u>know</u>. To fulfil their roles and responsibilities, leaders must undertake certain functions – by 'function' in this context we mean any behaviour, words or actions which meet one or more needs. Effectively applying these functions enable the leader's team to achieve its task and to hold the individual members of the team together as a working identity. Hence, the leader must be continually aware of meeting three distinct, but inter-connected, areas of need: those of:

- The task
- The team
- The individual

Task needs may include the imperative of clearly defined goals; a set of agreed priorities; and the availability of necessary resources. Team needs may be met by a workable structure of groups and, possibly, sub-groups; regular team meetings; and the appropriate allocation of roles to the groups. Whilst the needs of individual members of the teams may include relevant training and development; on-going support, perhaps including mentoring; and the equitable allocation of individual responsibilities. It is the leader's responsibility to meet all these various needs.

Specific actions, such as the examples in the preceding paragraph, can be grouped together into the broad functions a leader must apply. It is possible to list a significant number of leadership functions, although the ones I want to concentrate on here are:

- Planning
- Briefing
- Controlling
- Supporting
- Setting an example
- Reviewing

although it is not difficult to identify others, such as clarifying the task; informing; organising; evaluating; motivating etc.

The functions leaders must apply increase, both in number and complexity, as they rise through the three levels of leadership. Let us firstly consider those required of team leaders, and expand them with examples of how they relate to the needs of the task, team and individual.

Team Leaders' Functions

Planning. The team leader may, for example, be responsible for planning an evening function in a restaurant, or the preparation of a number of bedrooms in advance of a large party arriving at the hotel. The necessary resources will have to be identified and accessed, as well as timescales for their ordering and application. Sub-groups may have to be set up, with project leaders nominated, whilst the skills and knowledge of individual team members assessed and, if necessary, enhanced.

Briefing. Groups will have to be briefed on the task, with the team leader ensuring that all aspects are included. During the briefing the team should be given the opportunity to contribute to the discussion and offer suggestions. The leader should pay attention to each staff member, reading their body language to identify possible concerns or lack of understanding.

Controlling. During the execution of the task, the leader must continually check progress against the objectives and timescales contained within the plan. He or she should maintain supportive working practices, both within and between each team. The performance of each individual will be checked, with remedial action taken if required.

Supporting. All parties should be informed of progress as the task develops, celebrating success as milestones are passed. Open and effective inter-team communications and support will be essential to the success of the task and it is the team leader's responsibility to ensure this happens. Whilst supporting any team member who requires it, those who are coping well must still be encouraged and praised.

Setting an Example. Team leaders should be aware of the impact of their own body language, especially if problems occur during the task completion. If the task has been completed successfully, the leader should promote his or her team's success across the organisation. Setting a positive example will always be a motivational stimulus to all members of the team.

Reviewing. It is the responsibility of the leader to reflect on task outcomes at every stage and upon its completion, successful or not. The teams themselves should be involved in the review process, including the evaluation of any issues that impacted on team spirit. Reviewing the task may also identify individual development needs or, on the other hand, certain team members' potential for advancement within the organisation.

Operation Leaders' Functions

As team leaders progress in their careers they may take on greater leadership responsibilities that will contribute directly to the operation of their business. However, they will still have responsibility for the teams of people that report to them, hence will continue to have to carry out the team leadership functions outlined above. In fact, those functions are even more important at this level because the people who operational leaders oversee have teams of their own and will be heavily influenced by the way they, themselves, are led. Middle managers must not fall into the trap of simply thinking that, once they have acceded to that level, their team leadership responsibilities have changed – they have not: they have merely expanded to include others, such as:

Informing – gathering and communicating information up, down and at their own level within the organisation.

Interpreting – understanding and translating strategic and higher level operational decisions and requirements into language and activities which will be used at lower levels.

<u>Initiating</u> – creating, developing and putting into practice new initiatives, and supporting them within their areas of responsibility.

<u>Implementing</u> – putting the strategic plan into operation.

<u>Networking</u> – creating and building relationships with others, both within and outside the organisation.

<u>Influencing</u> – transforming the opinion of others, be they more senior members of the organisation or peers.

<u>Succession Planning</u> – ensuring on-going leadership provision within their department.

As with the list of team leadership functions, this list should be taken as illustrative, rather than exhaustive; but it does outline clearly the essential core of what operational leaders have to do, in addition to leading their immediate team. The functions predominantly relate to facilitating two-way communications and to using the authority vested in that enhanced level of leadership to make things happen. This essential 'engine room' work has to be achieved within the bounds of the organisation's policies, systems and constraints, as set at the strategic level. For example, this framework is likely to include financial parameters in the form of operating budgets, as well as less tangible requirements such as the imperative to operate within, and promote, a set of corporate values.

Operational leaders may be only one step removed from the day-to-day function of the business, such as a food and beverage manager who is responsible for kitchen, bar, restaurant and room service operations. Alternatively, he or she may report directly to the board, being responsible for an entire division. Whatever the case, the common factor of all operational leaders is that they should have direct engagement with both those who set the strategic agenda of the organisation, however small the requirement of that engagement may be, and those that oversee the service delivery to the end-user. They are the conduit through which information should flow upwards and downwards.

Strategic Leaders' Functions

Strategic leaders sit at, or very near to, the top of an organisation and have responsibility for the direction, purpose and success of the business. Their role involves defining the organisation's vision and values; determining the business strategy; and leading the operational team. Again, their role requires them to lead (senior) teams so the functions required of both team and operational leaders still apply. Additionally, however, they will be responsible for:

Providing direction for the organisation – creating a vision, defining corporate values, and ensuring that these are communicated throughout the organisation.

<u>Strategic planning</u> – making time for strategic thinking and policy planning.

<u>Exercising executive responsibility</u> – ensuring that the strategy is executed at operational levels by creating robust and effective administrative and people processes.

<u>Balancing the whole with its constituent parts</u> – organising, or re-organising, the organisation to ensure that it is fit for purpose.

<u>Releasing the corporate spirit</u> – building individual and team morale and confidence in order to release creative energy. Developing corporate culture in line with its values.

<u>Building relationships with all stakeholders</u> – including allies, partners, funders, political bodies and the broader society.

<u>Future leadership provision</u> – ensuring that policies are in place to identify and develop talent when recruiting new leaders, internally or externally.

For an example of the differing demands of operational and strategic leadership, and how one hospitality leader made that transition, see Graham Old's story at Chapter 2.4.

At this elevated level of leadership, responsibilities extend outside the bounds of the organisation as the demands of the wider society in which the organisation operates have to be considered. For example, strategic leaders will be responsible for due diligence and for ensuring that their organisation operates within the prevailing legal system at local, national or, perhaps, international levels. There are also moral and ethical considerations, not formally enshrined in law, but embodied in society's expectations of corporate behaviour. It is becoming increasing important for organisations to define expectations, and apply initiatives, under the banner of corporate social responsibility (CSR) – which will fall firmly within the functional responsibilities of their strategic leadership. CSR is explored in more depth in Chapter 1.4.

To conclude this chapter on the three approaches to leadership: all three have positive contributions to make to our understanding of this *mysterious and fascinating subject*, as John Adair describes it. However, none of them, alone, paints the complete picture. For example, in order for leaders to apply the <u>functions</u> associated with their level of authority they must have the knowledge necessary to apply them within the prevailing <u>situation</u>, as well as the generic leadership <u>qualities</u> to encourage and inspire their people to see them through to a successful outcome.

In concept, though, they do provide a solid platform for understanding and applying the principles and practice of effective leadership. In particular, the functional approach provides us with the foundation for meeting the needs of the task, the team and the individual – Action Centred Leadership, as expanded in the next chapter.

1.3 ACTION CENTRED LEADERSHIP

In the previous chapter we posed the question 'what makes a great leader' and considered three approaches to understanding it: Qualities, Situational and Functional. In summary, a leader is the sort of person with both the appropriate personal qualities and the necessary knowledge for a particular situation, and can apply the necessary functions to achieve a given task by means of a group of individuals working together as a team. In order to do this, the leader must ensure that the needs of the task, the team and each individual are fully met. Meeting these three needs is not a passive requirement: it requires the leader to determine exactly what the needs are, at any one time, and then take <u>actions</u> to fulfil them – hence the Action Centred Leadership (ACL) model.

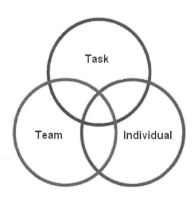

This 'three circles model' is perhaps the best-known and most widely used representation of the role of a leader in the world, since John Adair conceived and introduced it to industry in 1968. Since then it has been used as the basis of training courses delivered to more than one million managers and supervisors across the world. Many other models and theories have come and gone but ACL, represented by the three overlapping circles, has stood the test of time. Why is that? I believe it is because it offers a very simple, but not simplistic, practical template that leaders at all levels can apply for the benefit of their organisations.

From a lifetime's experience working in hospitality, in a range of sectors, I know that it is fundamentally a very practical industry. Meals are cooked; customers are served; support services such as housekeeping and porterage are undertaken – all by individuals applying their skills and taking appropriate actions. This does not take a great deal of deep thinking or academic theory. The front-line staff are practical people, led by practical team leaders who, over time, often take up more operational and strategic roles.

Hence, an approach to leadership and leadership development that is action-based, rather than theoretical, is, in my view, the most appropriate for our industry. As Albert Einstein proposed, *"Everything should be made as simple as possible, but not more simple"*. ACL offers a straightforward template upon which all leaders can inspire their staff to work together in teams to achieve their tasks.

The role of a team leader would, therefore, be:

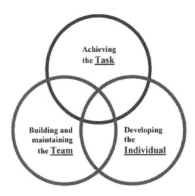

Operational leaders take on a greater level of leadership responsibility as they begin to contribute directly to the success of the organisation as a whole. Hence, their role is to take on a broader perspective, as represented within the appropriate circles as:

- Achieving the department task
- Building and maintaining the departmental culture
- Providing opportunities for individuals at a departmental level

whilst strategic leaders have overall accountability for the business: its direction, purpose and future success. Their roles, in terms of the task, team and individual, are therefore:

- Delivering the strategic vision
- Establishing and maintaining the organisational culture
- Ensuring opportunities for individual development

Returning to the three circles model as it refers to the requirement of a leader to meet the needs of the task, team and individual,

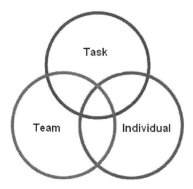

we note that the three circles overlap, demonstrating the point that each influences the other two. This is a fundamental feature of the model: that each of the needs must always be considered in relation to the other two. When a leader takes an action in order to contribute to a function, such as planning or briefing, he or she must consider its impact on all three circles. When planning a project, for example, the leader may decide to set targets for one, or more, individual involved in it. Will doing so impact positively or negatively on team cohesiveness and task completion?

Moreover, and perhaps more crucially, what will the effect be on the remaining two circles if the needs of the third are <u>not</u> met? If you imagine a disc eclipsing the task circle, symbolising a failure of the leader to meet the needs of the task,

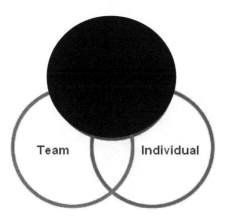

it becomes graphically apparent that doing so also impacts on the needs of team and the individual. Let us imagine that the task was to provide a private dinner for guests at a hotel but, due to the leader failing to plan it adequately, or perhaps brief the chefs and/or waiters appropriately, the event was a disaster. How would the staff feel and what would the effect be on the kitchen and restaurant teams?

Personally, I believe that the majority of workers actually want to do a good job, whatever their employment is. In this example, due to the leader's lack of planning and/or briefing, the staff concerned were not able to provide a good service to their customers. The customers were not satisfied – but neither were the chefs and waiters who wanted the event to be a great success. Hence, their individual needs were not met and so, as a consequence, they became dissatisfied and demotivated. This, in turn, impacts on how the team works as a whole: there is dissension in the ranks, the team begins to disintegrate, and if future tasks continue not to be completed satisfactorily, team members will seek better job satisfaction with other employers.

If team needs are not met by a leader who does not work hard to promote supportive working practices,

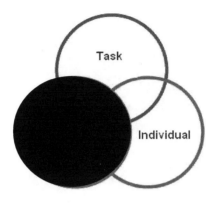

individual members become disenchanted and have no loyalty to their fellow group members. They will tend to adopt behaviours designed for their own benefit, rather than for the well-being and success of the team they belong to. Jealousies and conflict erupts within the group leading to 'point scoring' being more important than achievement. Clashes of personality and the forming of rival cliques make the fulfilment of the task increasingly difficult. Creativity and initiative are non-existent and absenteeism increases – all affecting the team's ability to meet the needs of the task.

Finally, a leader may be very task-oriented and keen to develop team working but fails to appreciate that, to do so, the needs of every individual within the team must be considered.

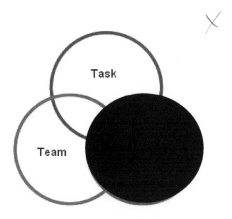

Teams are made up of individuals who, by the very nature of the term, all have different needs, concerns, ambitions, and motivational stimuli. The leader cannot, therefore, adopt a 'one size fits all' approach to team development. If, for example, individuals feel that they are not being given the necessary resources or development to do their jobs adequately, or perhaps are not being listened to when they voice their concerns in that respect, they will become frustrated and disinterested. Why should they work hard under such difficult circumstances to complete the tasks they are given? Gradually they shrink into their shells and withdraw co-operation from their fellow workers who, perhaps, they view as receiving preferential treatment from the leader.

Conversely, a leader that can affect a positive change in any of the three individual circles will see the benefit spread to the other two.

✓ A successfully completed task, the private dinner party perhaps, will build a sense of team identity, with each waiter and chef feeling that they have personally contributed to its success.

✓ High performing teams, by their very nature, consistently deliver the goods and contain highly motivated, loyal members who will always be willingly go that extra mile.

✓   <u>Individuals</u> who feel that they are valued for their contribution to both their team and the tasks they are asked to complete will add considerable value to the success of both areas.

The leader must, therefore, be aware of the needs of all three circles, but what will the effect be of focusing too heavily on one area of need? The model represents all three circles being the same size which may encourage us to assume that, in every situation, their needs are consistent and equal to each other. Whilst it is true that the three areas of needs are always present, that is not to say that, under certain situations, it may be necessary for the leader to focus heavily on one, even neglecting the others for short periods of time. Indeed, the demands of one need may be so overwhelming that the leader has to devote all his or her energies on it until the emergency is over. It is not too difficult to imagine scenarios where this could happen in our industry. All the power has been lost in the kitchen; you have lost half your dining room team due to a tummy bug; or one of your bar staff has just had a family bereavement – each example representing an overwhelming urgency for the leader to address the needs of the task, the team, or the individual.

Over extended periods of time, however, leaders should pay reasonably equal attention to each area of need. There are real dangers associated with concentrating on only one or two of them when there are needs present in those remaining, as we have previously identified.

I am sure that many of us have experienced people in leadership positions who are very task-oriented. The job comes first, 'it is only the bottom line that counts – people are paid to get on with their jobs; if they don't like it they can find somewhere else to work'! All the leader's energies are committed to ensuring the task is completed, at any cost. It is a fact that such an approach can pay dividends in the short term. But as Boris Yeltsin once said, *"You can build a throne of bayonets, but you cannot sit on it for long"*

A time will come when the leader is faced with one crisis too many, having pushed the team and its members too far, too often. If an organisation is to be successful over the long haul, individuals need to be fully developed and committed, working together productively as a team. The time will come when the leader who has focused so much attention on the needs of the task will find that the support of team members and the cohesiveness of the team(s) has simply evaporated to such an extent that he is standing alone, facing the consequences of his actions.

I have also known sectors of the hospitality industry where supervisors were so determined to create happy teams that, when circumstances changed, they were ill-prepared to cope with the resulting new demands. School catering is a very good example of this: prior to 1999, all the income generated from selling meals in all the schools within a local authority area went into one account, which subsequently paid the total costs associated with the provision – food, wages, equipment, marketing, administrative costs etc. Nobody knew if the meal service in individual schools were making a profit or loss; so long as the central account was achieving its targets, everyone was happy. There was little onus on the catering supervisors who managed school kitchens to concern themselves with the financial aspects of their roles. Hence, they tended to concentrate on keeping their staff happy in terms of wages and overtime, without being too concerned with the financial consequences. Being highly committed to their young customers, they saw their task as providing a good catering service, without too many financial concerns. Indeed, without profit and loss accounts for individual schools neither they, nor their managers, had the information needed to adopt a more financial perspective.

Then the Government introduced Fair Funding, which delegated the funds for the provision of their school meals service to individual head teachers. Moreover, the Heads did not have to purchase the service from the local authority – they could commission private catering contractors or elect to provide the service themselves in-house. From that moment, school catering entered the commercial, competitive marketplace at an individual school level. The task, as far as all the supervisors and managers were concerned, became very much more financially driven. The school catering supervisors now had to control their costs, especially labour costs, as never before, and often without adequate training to do so. Whilst they had previously, through no fault of their own, been relatively generous with the hours and overtime they gave their staff, now labour costs were heavily monitored and targets introduced. Having been involved in this sector from 1999 onwards, I can confirm that concentrating heavily on the team and individual needs, at the expense of the commercial element of the task, caused real problems for school catering leaders once the balance had to be adjusted accordingly. Understandably, morale was affected in many kitchens as staff found their take-home pay reduced.

In other examples, leaders can concentrate on individual needs; allowing staff too much latitude in a desire 'not to rock the boat'. Perhaps the leader favours the more dominant team members at the expense of those who are less confident or pushy. Yet those from the latter category will still form their own opinions and take action accordingly. Feeling badly treated and under-represented by their leader, they are likely to withdraw their support for both their team and their organisation as a whole.

Equally, the leader who is determined to have a 'happy ship' (another nautical metaphor, I am afraid) may spend too much time developing team working, at the expense of other business priorities. The regular team meetings and initiatives are increasingly viewed as a waste of time, covering the same old ground again and again. Achieving the task becomes secondary, whilst individuals become frustrated and, worse, worried about their jobs in the knowledge that sales and/or standards are in terminal decline.

So, as I have said, notwithstanding the imperative to react to short-term problems, leaders should pay reasonably equal attention to each area of need. That is, however, not the same as suggesting that the interventions of a leader should be equally divided between the three areas. The degree and frequency of interventions, or actions, in each circle will depend on the leader's assessment at the time. The best way of determining this is to stand back and consider, dispassionately and objectively, the whole picture. One useful way of envisaging this approach is as a helicopter hovering over the three circles. From this elevated vantage point the leader can assess each circle (need) and their interactions. So if, for example, there is a problem associated with the needs of the task, he or she can 'land' in that circle, address the need, and then take off again to reassess the whole picture. Leaders must develop the ability to detach themselves from the nitty-gritty of the operation, without losing an appreciation of every aspect of it; homing in to meet any identified need; and then regaining their detached position in order to deploy their efforts in the most effective way as the need arises.

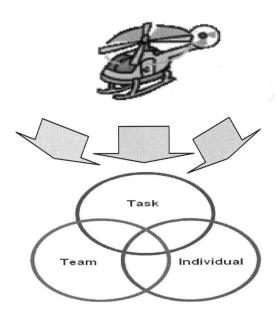

I hope it is becoming apparent that ACL requires, not only to have the generic <u>qualities</u> of inspirational leadership and the knowledge required to address each <u>situation</u>, but also the ability to take actions to fulfil the <u>functions</u> of a leaders role, at every level.

In the previous chapter we concentrated on the following functions, whilst accepting that the list is by no means exhaustive:

- Planning
- Briefing
- Controlling
- Supporting
- Setting an example
- Reviewing

Also, fundamental to the concept of ACL is that actions taken in furtherance of these functions must be directed at meeting the needs of the task, the team, and the individual. There follows a list of actions that provides a useful aide-memoir for leaders determined to ensure they meet all three needs when fulfilling either a single function (for example, when briefing their team) or when undertaking several functions, as part of a more comprehensive project:

PLANNING

<u>Task</u> needs:
- Set success criteria for every stage
- Devise contingency plan
- Source and consider relevant experience outside team
- Ensure clarity of vision
- Consider all courses of action
- Identify required resources
- Set time milestones

- Create training plan to support task completion
- Identify potential hurdles and/or blockages

Team needs:

- Allocate roles to teams and/or sub-groups
- Appoint project/group leaders
- Use any existing specialist groups to meet objectives
- Set team objectives
- Consider most effective constitution of teams
- Be aware of any personal issues when constituting teams

Individual needs:

- Consider individual skills and experience
- Identify any specialist knowledge
- Involve individuals in planning process
- Set individual targets and objectives
- Identify any development needs

BRIEFING

Task needs:

- Include all aspects of task
- Share your vision
- Keep it simple
- Break task down into constituent parts
- Consider who needs what information
- Plan and practice delivery
- Use props, if appropriate
- Be open and honest

Team needs:

- Encourage suggestions
- Focus briefing on team roles and responsibilities
- Be prepared to amend plan as result of team input

- Remain open-minded
- Stress importance of inter/intra-team co-operation
- Ensure all team members have the opportunity to contribute to briefing discussion
- Do not allow more vocal team members to dominate or side-track discussion

Individual needs:

- Check understanding
- Stress benefits of achieving task
- Be prepared to amend plan as a result of individual input
- Recognise resistance to change
- Read body language
- Seek buy-in
- Adopt appropriate questioning techniques
- Reassure any concerns
- Stress individual contribution to task success

CONTROLLING

Task needs:

- Stand back to assess progress
- Introduce control systems
- Retain overall control
- Adopt 'helicopter' approach
- Do not get too personally involved
- Delegate, as appropriate
- Continually check progress against objectives and milestones

Team needs:

- Maintain supportive working practices
- Be aware of any inter/intra-team issues
- Ensure each group receives the support it needs from other teams

- Ensure each team is meeting its objectives at every milestone
- Assess whether group leaders are fulfilling their roles
- Hold regular team meetings

Individual needs:

- Encourage self-discipline
- Check performance of each individual
- Take appropriate remedial action, if required
- Adopt an open-door policy
- Do not allow dominant individuals to hinder task completion
- Be prepared to re-allocate individual roles and responsibilities

SUPPORTING

Task needs:

- Keep all parties informed of progress
- Provide additional resources, as required
- Celebrate achievement of milestones
- Hold regular update meetings
- Consider need for external specialist support

Team needs:

- Address any conflicts between teams
- Ensure each team appreciates how they depend on other groups
- Ensure open and effective inter-team communications
- Arrange visits to other groups or establishments if advantageous
- Use personal authority to protect teams from malign external influences

Individual needs:

- Assist and encourage individuals
- Make time to speak to each team member
- Address individual concerns
- Act as coach and mentor
- Provide additional support, as required
- Set up 'buddy' support, if needed
- Identify individual motivational stimuli
- Do not ignore those coping effectively, whilst supporting those that are not

SETTING AN EXAMPLE

Task needs:

- Lead from the front
- Be aware of personal body language
- Be motivated yourself
- Keep calm if faced with problems
- Be open to constructive criticism
- Be visible throughout task completion
- Face up to conflict and problems
- Ensure your people know you remain accountable

Team needs:

- Share in team experience
- Use customer-facing teams to demonstrate task benefits to other teams
- Celebrate team success
- Promote your team successes across the organisation
- Act as a team player yourself
- Be involved at key stages to demonstrate personal commitment

Individual needs:

- Always portray positive appearance
- Assess impact of your own body language

- Demonstrate your trust, confidence and support
- Be a role model
- Continually reinforce benefits of task completion
- Check that group leaders are also fulfilling all the above actions

REVIEWING

Task needs:

- Reflect on outcomes at every stage
- Assess consequences of every action taken
- Be aware of any unnecessary bureaucracy
- Use objective measurements whenever possible
- Undertake cost-benefit analysis
- Identify communication blockages
- Be prepared to amend initial plan, if necessary
- Allocate additional resources, if required

Team needs:

- Evaluate team spirit
- Assess how teams are working together
- Identify any negative inter/intra-team issues
- Involve teams in reviewing progress
- Involve teams in evaluating final result
- Consider if group sizes and constitution are still appropriate for task

Individual needs:

- Review individual development needs during task completion
- Involve individuals in reviewing progress
- Involve individuals in evaluating final results
- Agree future performance targets
- Address any shortcomings affecting team/task needs
- Identify any leadership skills demonstrated during task completion

- Consider amending roles and responsibilities during task completion
- Consider if any more able team members could support those less so.

1.4 THE TWENTY-FIRST CENTURY LEADER

State of the Nation

Before we look ahead to the demands facing hospitality leaders as the century unfolds, we should establish where the industry currently stands. The Sector Skills Council for the hospitality, leisure, travel and tourism (HLTT) industry, People 1st's *State of the Nation Report 2009* offered a detailed analysis of labour trends, education and training. It contained the following factors that should influence the approach of twenty-first century hospitality leaders:

- The HLTT industries combine to play an important role in the UK economy, employing around two million people and accounting for one in 14 UK jobs.

- Fortunes across the industry have varied over the past five years, with the restaurant sector's workforce increasing by nine per cent. Conversely, the licensed sector has suffered badly during 2008/09, with pubs now closing almost ten times faster than in 2006.

- Sixteen per cent of the industry's workforce is aged between 16 and 19, whilst only five per cent are over 60 years of age.

- Whilst 59 per cent of the workforce is female, the number of women holding senior leadership positions is low, and is falling.

Over half the women workers are part-time, compared to 31 per cent of men.

- Between February 2008 and February 2009 the number of registered unemployed people looking for work in the HLTT industries rose from 47,875 to 75,345. This now equates to nearly two job seekers for every vacancy.

- Labour turnover across the whole sector is higher than any other within the UK economy and, despite the economic downturn, rose from 30 per cent in 2005 to 31 per cent in 2008. It is estimated that HLTT employees spent £414 million on recruiting and developing new staff in 2008/09.

- Approximately 19 per cent of all vacancies are proving hard to fill due to a shortage of skilled applicants, with chefs being the hardest to recruit.

- Slightly more HLTT employers are now training their staff, although much of this training is informal and less than a third of employers have a formal training budget.

- Management skills appear to be improving, as indicated by the fact that the proportion of employers reporting that their managers lack the required skills fell four per cent, to 26 per cent, between 2005 and 2007.

- Customer service skills have been identified as the main skill shortage within the current workforce, although there are signs of improvement in that area.

- Improvements to service standards could, in part, be due to the high number of Accession State workers entering the HLTT industry, especially within hospitality, as employers value them for their good customer service ethic. However, as fewer migrant workers are now entering the industry, and many are returning home, resulting in employers becoming more reliant on the indigenous population, there is a danger that customer service levels could fall in the future.

- The recession is forcing more employers to think about cutting costs. It is therefore more important than ever that employers have credible retention strategies to retain skilled and valued staff and thus reduce unnecessary recruitment costs.

- Fifty-one per cent of HLTT employers are planning to reduce staff training as a result of the recession, whilst 25 per cent are planning to increase it.

- The long-term prediction for the HLTT industry is for it to grow and remain an important contributor to the UK economy.

- Total employment is forecast to grow by nearly ten per cent (208,000 additional posts) by 2017. When replacement demand is taken into account, projections indicate that a total of 1,063,000 additional people will be required in the ten years to 2017.

- The sector continues to be over-reliant on a shrinking pool of younger workers – with 48 per cent currently under the age of 30, compared to 18 per cent across the whole of the economy.

- Many young people and Eastern European migrants working in the HLTT industry are transient workers, thus contributing to high levels of labour turnover. When the economy recovers and recruitment levels increase, employers that seek to employ workers who are more likely to stay longer with the business, such as older workers and women returning to work, could improve staff retention rates thereby reducing recruitment and induction costs.

- In the introduction to this report, Brian Wisdom, Chief Executive of People 1st makes two further points:

❖ The three main skill priorities (management and leadership; customer service; and chef skills) identified in 2007 remain unchanged and the 2009 State of the Nation Report underlines their significance. Indeed, the recession intensifies their importance, with the former two likely to become even more critical as competition increases for a declining customer base.

❖ Improving people management skills and staff retention will be one way to reduce costs as labour turnover across the sector remains high and is a costly problem.

Industry Changes

So far within the twenty-first century we have seen certain organisational changes in companies across the UK. Organisations are generally getting larger, either through organic growth or by merger, and increasingly compete and develop on an international stage. Labour mobility across countries, even continents, is becoming the norm, with an increasing percentage of an organisation's workforce not being born in the country it operates in. Hence, work teams are likely to be influenced by a wide cultural diversity. This is a particular factor within the hospitality industry where it is not unusual for a large London hotel to have representatives of over 40 nationalities within its staff.

Service providers are increasingly influenced by their customers' ever-greater expectations of the products and services they purchase. Moreover, customers are more willing to change suppliers than before, especially if they believe that the provider does not recognise their importance. Hence, services are becoming more customer-driven and the front-line staff, who ultimately influence the customer's perception of the company as a whole, are being recognised by the more forward-thinking organisations as the principle key to their success.

As part of The Hospitality Leadership Excellence Survey (Appendix B), I asked the leaders I interviewed what industry-specific issues placed demands upon hospitality leaders. Whilst they suggested a number of different factors, there was consensus on the following:

- The industry does not have a good reputation for leadership and this can deter people from entering the industry.

- The environment is very competitive, so you have to create a culture for staff that creates loyalty to the brand.

- Due to the volatility of the industry, both good and bad times have to be managed, so you need to be an effective leader for both.

- You have to be able to lead a very diverse workforce, and often one that is geographically spread, with the lowest paid acting as the principal ambassadors for the company. It takes a particular type of leadership to be able to motivate everyone.

Also, when asked to consider if there were any changes to the industry that would pose leadership challenges in the future, the interviewees suggested that the following factors were likely to have an impact:

- A struggle for quality staff in transient labour markets.

- Further industry consolidation and brand competition.

- Increasing level of competition.

- Higher customer demands.

- More people working in the industry coming from outside of the sector.

- An influx of workers from EU countries.

Each of these creates different leadership demands in terms of how people are recruited, managed, and motivated to bring out the best in the industry.

In addition to the organisational changes experienced by UK companies over recent years, employees themselves have changed in terms of their profile, attitude and expectations. The younger generation entering the employment market do not look for, or expect, a job for life to the extent that previous generations did. They are more likely to have planned their career progression for many years ahead, which may include changing employment every few years.

In periods of low unemployment, employees will not be grateful to have a job as in previous generations and will certainly be more aware of their increased value to an employer. In the light of this perception, staff have increasingly high expectations of their employer and expect to be offered a range of benefits, including development training. Moreover, they may require more flexible working arrangements to provide a better work-life balance. Whilst it is true to say that the recession has reversed or slowed some of these trends, there is no reason to assume that post-recession leaders will not have to face these challenges anew.

If the recent influx of workers from the Accession States and elsewhere continues after the recession, leaders will continue to have very multi-national teams, with the inherent cultural differences having to be identified and managed. Martina Dudasova, herself a Czech, offers an interesting insight into leading a team of mixed nationalities within a hotel environment in Chapter 2.12. Eastern European workers, whilst being valued greatly for their customer service and work ethic by hospitality employers, often do require a different leadership approach from the British staff they work alongside, as explained by Graham Baker in Chapter 2.10. For example, 'home-grown' workers are much less likely to automatically respect their manager merely due to the position he or she holds. They may well have researched their employment rights and will be prepared to question decisions and company policy they feel is inappropriate or unjust.

Conversely, whilst some foreign migrant workers may well be over-qualified for the duties they are performing in British companies, their cultural backgrounds influence them to adopt a more deferential attitude towards their managers. Some Far Eastern workers, and some from Eastern Europe, find it difficult, for example, to call their team leader by his or her first name. In their home countries people in managerial capacities are afforded automatic respect – whether they deserve it or not. Building relationships with those having inherent hierarchical leanings can be a difficult, but ultimately most rewarding, challenge for leaders, especially at the team level.

Leadership Theories and Practice

Up to the 1930s, leadership was considered an inherent gift which some fortunate people, generally from the elite social classes, received by virtue of their birth – the 'Great Man' Theory. Then US social psychologists began studying groups of people and found that democratic leadership was not only possible, it was more effective. Thus, a more egalitarian view evolved from the elitist and sexist previous thinking. Unfortunately, however, the research indicated that the practice of leadership that was most successful in small groups was not transferable to large groups or organisations.

The Second World War encouraged academics to try to identify what traits leaders needed to have in order to influence people into action, although their research produced no consensus on the key traits necessary for effective leadership. Indeed, in the 1950s Ralph Stogdill compared the results of various studies attempting to establish the Trait Theory and found them contradictory and inconclusive.

Stogdill and others then turned their attentions to how leaders behaved, especially towards their followers. They moved from the personalities to the practice of leadership. Hence, during the 1950s and 1960s behavioural theories became the favoured approach to leadership within organisations. Different patterns of behaviour were grouped together and labelled as management styles.

During this time certain psychologists, largely American again, formed theories about how, by understanding the fundamental motivational stimuli that affect people, leaders can inspire them to greater effort. Perhaps the most famous motivational theories were Maslow's Hierarchy of Needs, Hertzberg's Hygiene Factors, and McGregor's X-Y Theory. Interestingly, I believe that these theories continue to hold water today – proving that the fundamental principles of leadership have not changed so much over the past 50 years.

Yet over that time so many leadership theories have emerged, including: contingency model leadership; transactional leadership; situational leadership, transformational leadership; directive leadership; continuum of leadership; Level 5 leadership; Six Sigma; Seven Habits; authentic leadership; participative leadership; path-goal theory; multi-dimensional model; servant leadership; and many more, I am sure!

Enduring Principles of Inspirational Leadership

As I have previously said, I do not believe that the principles of inspirational leadership have changed greatly over recent decades. They can, I propose, be condensed into the standards underpinning the six pieces of my own leadership model, The Leadership Jigsaw.

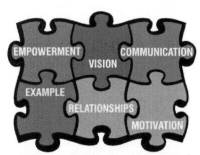

The Leadership Jigsaw

namely:

✓ A leader builds supportive <u>relationships</u>
✓ A leader sets an <u>example</u>
✓ A leader is a <u>visionary</u>
✓ A leader understands what <u>motivates</u> each team member
✓ A leader <u>empowers</u> others to reach their potential
✓ A leader understands the power of <u>communications</u>

In practical terms, the enduring principles of inspirational leadership, notwithstanding any theory or model, require a leader to:

- Promote team development.
- Identify and remove blockages to effective communications.
- Be aware of internal and external resistances to change.
- Promote a positive, supportive working environment – both within teams and between teams.

- Celebrate individual and team successes at every opportunity.
- Be open and approachable.
- Treat people as individuals, who have individual needs.
- Recognise and reward good performance.
- Ensure consistency and equality of treatment.
- Create a culture of honesty and transparency.
- Provide enjoyable, interesting and rewarding work.
- Ensure a fair pay structure is applied to all.

The Twenty-First Century Hospitality Leader

The previous list of leadership principles is, I believe, as relevant now as ever before. However, as we have seen, the hospitality industry is changing and so we must consider how twenty-first century hospitality leaders must rise to future challenges (some of which are identified in the additional research findings at Appendix B).

Promote your organisation as a good company to join. People 1st estimates that employment is forecast to grow by over 200,000 posts by 2017 and will continue to be over-reliant on a shrinking pool of younger workers. Hence, if organisations are to compete in this demanding labour market they must be seen as employers of choice for all categories of staff; from graduates to casual, part-time employees. Being recognised in awards, such as the Caterer and Hotelkeeper's 'Best Places to Work in Hospitality' can be very influential at a national level, but so can inspirational team leadership at unit level – such as demonstrated by the two champions from McDonald's Restaurants in Part II of this book.

Encourage staff to see their long-term future with the organisation. In addition to recruiting quality staff, they must also be retained. It has been estimated that the average cost of recruiting and training a new employee is £1,500. Moreover, as companies cannot afford a continual drain of staff they have trained and nurtured, additional effort will be required as the century unfolds to win employee commitment and involvement. Their increasing demand for developmental training and flexible working arrangements will have to be met if they are to see their long term future with the company. As brand competitiveness increases, those companies whose staff are most loyal and committed will enjoy a distinct advantage.

Address the industry's negative reputation. The hospitality industry, in particular, is perceived by some to offer bad conditions of employment, including long, unsocial hours; low pay; and aggressive management. This inevitably affects its attraction, in particular for younger job hunters and their advisors. Leaders should do whatever they can to promote the industry as one offering the potential for job satisfaction and excellent career development opportunities, including the potential to work overseas. They should work with industry bodies, as well as local schools, career advisors and parents to dispel its negative reputation.

Create a positive, multi-cultural working environment. Hospitality managers will continue to lead a multi-cultural and very diverse workforce. Current levels of labour mobility are unlikely to reduce, thus the challenge of identifying the motivational stimuli of each individual from every cultural background will continue.

Change from being a 'boss' to being a team player and a coach to team members. Old authoritarian styles of management are becoming redundant as employees expect to be recognised and respected for the contribution they make to their organisation. The key to building supportive relations between leader and follower will increasingly be mutual respect, rather than the application of power.

React to the impact of external influences. The hospitality industry is particularly prone to the effects of external influences – be they of great magnitude, like a global recession or a terrorist attack such as 9/11; or more localised, such as an outbreak of food poisoning and the negative media interest that inevitably follows. Successful leaders will have contingency plans in place to react swiftly to difficult trading situations and will be adaptable and flexible enough to ensure the continuing success of their businesses.

Empower front-line staff to exceed customers' expectations. With customers expecting ever-higher standards of product and service, leaders must recognise that it is those that serve them who are in a position to make them satisfied or dissatisfied; return or never come again. They must be given the authority to make decisions that will delight the customer and, thus, differentiate their company from its competitors. Yet it is usually the lowest paid employees who are potentially the greatest ambassadors of their company. Leaders must, therefore, find ways of inspiring them without, necessarily, offering additional financial reward. One way would certainly be to trust them to get on with their jobs without overbearing supervision.

Share business goals with employees. If leaders, at all levels, are to encourage their employees to join them on their journey, then staff need to know where they are going. Employee engagement will be increasingly important as companies strive to develop their business in post-recession Britain, and beyond. If leaders don't explain where the business is pointed and what it is seeking to achieve, how can people know how they are meant to contribute? Yet, a recent Government survey identified that only one in four employees said that their management had clearly communicated the company's business objectives. Some hospitality organisations, such as Radisson Edwardian Hotels and Marriott, have an open communication culture where all members of their staff have access to virtually all information relating to the company. This is a lead that other hospitality organisations would do well to emulate.

Introduce Corporate Social Responsibility (CSR) policies. Society, including customers of hospitality providers, is increasingly becoming aware of the environmental impact of business activities. As terms such as 'carbon footprint' become more widely used and understood, our industry will be subjected to ever-greater scrutiny to ensure it is acting in an environmentally sound fashion. Hence, industry leaders must carefully consider the impact their operations have, both on the environment and on their customers' perceptions.

Many HLTT organisations have introduced CSR policies, which are defined by the Confederation of British Industry as *'the acknowledgement by companies that they should be accountable, not only for their financial performance, but for the impact of their activities on society and/or the environment'*.

Essentially, CSR embraces the concepts of:

- <u>Trading responsibly</u> – providing transparent information about all aspects of the business operation and working against corruption and exploitation.

- <u>Protecting the environment</u> – by innovating; implementing eco-efficiency measures; investing in technologies; and promoting conservation.

- <u>Working in partnership with communities</u> – by avoiding exploitative practices and providing economic and social benefits.

- <u>Providing information to inform stakeholders</u> – including customers, to help them make value-based choices.

Not only will sound and well-communicated CSR policies meet the needs and increasing expectations of twenty-first century customers, they can improve and sustain financial performance. Hilton Europe, for example, achieved energy savings of ten per cent across its 80 hotels as a result of its *'We Care'* environmental programme. In many instances, resource savings can be achieved for very little investment. Chapter 2.6 includes an overview of Brookwood Partnership's *Planet Matters* initiative that they adopt within the school catering sector.

The Institute of Hospitality's Hospitality Climates Energy Efficiency Programme has attracted over 6,000 hospitality business since its launch in 2000, most of whom have reduced their energy costs by a considerable amount, whilst maintaining their focus on good customer service and profitability. As the Institute's Chief Executive, Philippe Rossiter, explains, *"The success of Hospitality Climates has been due to the seamless connection between operational activity and the introduction of energy saving measures. In other words, it has become part of the business's culture, and is not regarded as a resource-intensive 'add-on', but as an integral part of the good management of all resources".*

Looking forward, all industry leaders should seriously consider the benefits, environmentally and in terms of their customers' changing expectations, of adapting their operational procedures to embrace environmental best practice.

In Summary

To summarise this chapter: twenty-first century hospitality leaders must not only apply the generic and enduring principles of inspirational leadership, but they must also be aware of, and react to, future industry and employment trends in order to ensure the continuing success of their organisations as the century unfolds. The requirements of all those involved within HLTT, providers and consumers alike, will, over time, change and, hence, our leaders' approach must change in response to them.

1.5 GROWING HOSPITALITY LEADERS

You will remember from Chapter 1.1 that Professor Arvey from the University of Minnesota conducted a study of 325 pairs of twins and, as a result, found that around 70 per cent of leadership skills are acquired by environmental influences such as training, job experience and education; with the remaining affected by our genetic make-up. Hence, leaders are neither entirely born nor made. Understanding this should influence organisations' approach to the selection and development of leaders at all levels. Recruitment and selection of leaders should be based upon a clear understanding of the leadership qualities, attitude and experience required of the post to be filled and, thereafter, a range of development activities applied to 'grow' the successful applicant into the post and, hopefully, into others at higher levels of leadership.

In the UK, there are centres set up to develop leaders in every aspect of public and commercial life, whilst in the birthplace of current leadership thinking, the USA, an estimated 40 billion dollars are spent on leadership development every year. However, John Adair suggests that a significant amount of this money is misdirected as it is often largely spent on the top ten to twenty per cent of the organisations' workforce, whilst the development needs of the leaders at other levels are largely ignored. Moreover, to compound the problem, he has found that directors, chief executives and even people running the leadership programmes, such as HR, are often not clear about their required content and approach. *"Many have never had experience of training leaders and that means their knowledge base is shaky – they never really know what works and what doesn't so they have to get it out of books and conferences"*, he says. *"I'm a great believer that you should come up through the ranks and do your time actually training or instructing people in leadership. You can work on being a strategist later on"*.

Change is the key theme here. Despite the fact that so many leadership programmes are disappointing, it has not diminished the desire to put leadership high on the agenda. Nor has it, paradoxically, dampened the impetus of the worldwide revolution for management and leadership.

"Change throws up leaders <u>and</u> leaders bring about change. If your organisation exists in a sort of isolation ward, without any form of change troubling you, then don't bother with leadership – just carry on the way you are. However, that is not a luxury that most organisations can afford".

It is certainly not the case that the hospitality industry has been, or will in the foreseeable future, be immune from change. Yet, whilst there are some exceptional examples of industry organisations that take leadership development seriously, People 1st reports that in the Hospitality, Leisure, Tourism and Travel industry only 40 per cent of organisations trained their employees in management and/or leadership in the twelve months preceding its *State of the Nation Report 2009*, with the hospitality sector being less active in this respect than travel and tourism.

Selection of Leaders

The recruitment of people to fill leadership positions at all levels depends both on selecting a person who has the potential to grow into the role <u>and</u> giving him or her the support needed to fulfil their potential. Far too often, in the hospitality industry as in others, one or both of these essential pre-requisites to effective leadership are missing. Selecting people to fill leadership positions will essentially be by one of two methods:

Internal Selection. Here, people will be promoted to a leadership position from within the organisation they currently work. They may have applied for the more senior position or, as is often the case, have been persuaded to take up the role due to operational pressures in that unit. If that is the case, time may not allow the application of an appropriate selection process. Indeed, the person may be given the role, possibly on a short term basis, without competition from other candidates.

External Selection. Here, applications are invited from those not currently working for the organisation. These may be people entering the industry for the first time; direct from further or higher education; or from those currently working for another organisation in the same, or other, sectors.

It should be noted also that, on occasions, selecting people for a leadership position within an organisation may involve both internal and external applicants. Whichever method is applied, the implications of choosing someone who is unable to take up, or grow into, a leadership position can be dramatic in terms of the task, the team he or she will be leading, and the individual members of that team. The implications are wide-ranging and, in pure financial terms, they can be very significant. Employing leaders who cannot deliver the task has obvious financial implications, as can the effect they will have on staff turnover within the team. A survey by a training and consultancy company in the hospitality industry, Learn Purple, identified that 57 per cent of people leaving their jobs in our industry cited poor leadership as the reason for them doing so! Bearing this in mind, it is surely essential that organisations take sufficient care and attention in selecting the right person to take up a leadership position.

The process should involve several stages. The Four Seasons hotel group ensures that every applicant, not only for leadership positions, is interviewed by four separate managers – from the person who will be the successful applicant's line manager, through to the general manager of the hotel. Whilst the more junior interviewers will be seeking to assess skills and knowledge, the more senior managers will be more interested in attitudinal characteristics. The hotel group believe that, whilst skills and knowledge can be taught and developed on the job, the applicant's attitudinal qualities are more fundamental and are much more difficult to change after the person has taken up the post.

Yet in the hospitality industry, attitude, especially in relation to customer relations, is absolutely critical to the success of the operation. Far too often, people are recruited based on existing skills and knowledge, but subsequently struggle or are dismissed due to inappropriate attitudes. One way of objectively testing attitudes is via the application of a psychometric test. After being recruited to lead the hospitality department at Aston University I was invited to take a psychological test that was designed to evaluate my general IQ, which I thought at the time was rather inappropriate for the non-academic role I was about to take up. More recently, I was invited to take a test designed to evaluate my temperament, disposition and attitude. I found these results to be particularly accurate and illuminating and believe that such a test should be considered when recruiting people for a leadership role in our industry as it definitely shed light on, in this case, my likelihood to work effectively both as a team leader, and within a team. Hence, from my personal experience, psychological profiling can be a useful component of a leadership selection process, so long as it seeks to measure appropriate leadership-related skills, as opposed to the candidate's IQ.

In addition to an interview-based process, it is also important that the employer has an opportunity to assess potential leaders in a group situation similar to the one they would take up were they to be engaged. Doing so is surely the only realistic way of assessing the person's leadership potential for achieving the task, leading the team and dealing with team members at an individual level. I am not suggesting that all applicants should be assessed in this practical way: more likely, only those who make it to the final stage of the selection process.

As far as internal applicants are concerned, giving them the chance to undertake a leader's role should not be too difficult as in-house arrangements could be made to facilitate this. Offering external candidates such an opportunity would be more difficult – although not impossible: the application of a trial period of employment would be one way of doing so.

I also believe that part of the assessment of a potential leader working in a group situation should be made by the staff themselves. The people the applicant is leading during the trial period should be asked for their assessment of that person's performance in terms of the task, the team and the individual. It is surely crucial to gain the views of team members, in addition to those at a more senior level, prior to the confirmation of the applicant's appointment.

Unfortunately, it is my experience that often, especially in the public sector, a general assistant, for example, who is undertaking her duties with enthusiasm and capability is moved into the kitchen manager's role if it becomes available. This often happens from within the team in which she is working – thus making the transition into her leadership role even more difficult. It may be that this internal promotion is appropriate and has the potential to succeed, but the new team leader must be given appropriate development training and support if she is to undertake her role effectively. Far too often, this is not the case: any training follows many months later, if at all! Not only is this person not given help to grow into the role but often her subsequent performance is not evaluated by her line managers – thus failing to take the opportunity to assess her in a real life group situation, as I proposed earlier.

So what should we be looking for when assessing someone's potential as a leader? John Adair proposes the following behaviours, grouped under five headings, which could also be used as the foundation of a leadership evaluation process:

1. Leadership and team work – the ability to get things going – especially the ability to get people working well as a team towards a common goal. Typical behaviours being:

    - Sets direction and initiates action.
    - Plans and organises.
    - Delegates responsibility.
    - Coordinates and controls.
    - Shows sensitivity to needs and feelings of individuals.
    - Motivates and encourages others.
    - Sets group standards.
    - Disciplines where necessary.
    - Seeks help and advice.
    - Plays positive role as team member.

2. Decision-making abilities – the ability to think clearly in order to be able to solve problems and make decisions. Typical behaviour being:

    - Analyses problems.
    - Shows reasoning and logical thinking.
    - Is 'swift on the uptake'.
    - Thinks imaginatively and creatively.
    - Has a sense of reality.
    - Has 'helicopter' ability to stand back.
    - Demonstrates good judgement.
    - Has an inquiring mind.
    - Generates solutions.
    - Is decisive when required.

3. <u>Communication abilities</u> – the ability to make points so that others understand them, and to comprehend the points that others make. Typical behaviours include:

- Speaks audibly and clearly.
- Uses simple and concise language.
- Communicates on paper easily and well.
- Listens to others with perception.
- Reads with speed and comprehension.
- Argues assertively, but not aggressively.
- Chairs a meeting well.
- Ensures good group communications, upwards, downwards and sideways.
- Shows awareness of non-verbal communication.
- Gets others enthusiastic about his or her ideas.

4. <u>Self-management abilities</u> – the ability to manage your time effectively and to organise yourself well. Typical behaviours include:

- A self-motivator – 'lights his or her own fire'
- Able to work on own initiative with little supervision
- Sets and achieves challenging goals.
- Works to deadlines.
- Makes good use of his or her own time.

5. <u>Personal qualities</u> – the following qualities (in no order of merit) are mentioned as being of value by employers:

- Enthusiasm.
- Integrity.
- Strong, but not dominating, personality.
- Personal impact, good appearance, poise.
- Resilience, ability to work under pressure.
- Flexibility and adaptability.

- Self-confidence or self-assurance.
- Reliability, stability, calmness.
- Breadth of interest.

LEADERSHIP TRAINING

I made the point in the previous section that, following the selection of an appropriate person to hold a leadership post, there should follow an appropriate amount of leadership development. Too often the people are left to sink or swim in their new role without the application of any subsequent training. It is a sad fact that leadership training, indeed training of any nature, is not always seen as a high priority, including within the hospitality industry. Remember that People 1st, our Sector Skills Council, identified that 33 per cent of hospitality employers are not undertaking any staff training and, shockingly, 25 per cent said that nothing would get them to train their staff! No doubt many employers see training as an unnecessary expense. Perhaps they should consider the old maxim, *'If you think training is expensive, try ignorance!'*

Indeed, within higher education in our industry I believe that only one university currently offers a hospitality degree with the world 'leadership' in the title. There are scores of courses training students to be hospitality managers, but few training for hospitality leadership. Yet the leaders that I interviewed in the Hospitality Leadership Excellence Survey identified a significant shortcoming in leadership development within our industry. One commented *"Are we attracting sufficient talent and are we developing and preparing that talent to do the leadership job that is required? I suspect we are not."* One of the outcomes from the research identified a significant shortfall in leadership training in our industry, both at team leader and at operational leader level.

Leadership training in an organisation is often the result of someone in a senior position, perhaps the chief executive or the HR director, deciding that 'leadership is a good thing and we need more of it'. Thus the impetus for a leadership development initiative is spawned and action is required. Hospitality organisations and their leaders are practical by nature and are used to reacting swiftly to external pressures. However, to develop a leadership development strategy without sufficient thought and preparation may result in the following outcomes:

- There is no clear concept of what leadership actually is and how it should relate to, and combine with, good management.

- There is no understanding of the different levels of leadership and the different requirements of each in terms of development.

- Commitment, and sometimes even a degree of interest, is lacking at the top of the organisation.

- Programmes may reflect the latest leadership fad or fashion, rather than understanding and applying the founding principles of enduring leadership effectiveness.

- Organisers look for instant results from the development programmes and when it fails to materialise they move on to embrace the next 'panacea'.

Organisations that do not take the time to consider leadership in its broadest sense may adopt the unconscious assumption that leadership development is something that starts and stops with senior management. Perhaps they send their senior people to prestigious business schools or arrange expensive one-to-one mentoring schemes. Yet I contend that, in the hospitality industry in particular, the natural starting point for leadership development is with team leaders. It is, after all, team leaders who are in a position to inspire front-line staff to provide excellent customer service. As many of those I interviewed for my research commented *'happy staff, mean happy customers, mean good business'.* Moreover, team leadership is the principal seedbed for an organisation's operational leaders and they, in turn, should be the natural source of its strategic leaders. So, if you lay the right foundation at the lower levels you will reap the rewards throughout the organisation. In practical terms, it is also often the case that it is easier to require all newly appointed team leaders to attend a course than it is to get operational and strategic leaders to do so.

Team leader training courses, like Hospitality Leadership's *Certificate in Team Leadership* (Appendix C), should be short (two days ideally) and delivered by a properly qualified trainer who can relate its principles to the working environment of the delegates. The hallmark of such training is that it should be simple, practical, relevant, varied and challenging. Supervisors and junior managers employed in the hospitality industry are, by and large, practical people who relate best to training that offers an opportunity 'to learn by doing'. Hence it should have short, pacy presentations or group discussions, interspersed between practical leadership exercises. There is no doubt that effective leadership skills <u>can</u> be taught so long as the training meets these criteria. As John Adair says, the basic principle in leadership development is that *"an organisation should never give a team leadership role or position to someone without training. We don't entrust our children to bus drivers who are not trained; why place any kind of worker under leaders who have no training?".*

Many problems associated with leadership development at the lower levels are apparent in public sector catering: team leaders promoted to their posts to fill operational contingencies; a lack of leadership development training offered; very little assessment of their performance in the period following their promotion; and, very often, general assistants promoted to lead a team in their own kitchens. One of the initial hurdles trainers have to overcome is to get these ladies to appreciate that they actually <u>are</u> leaders! Many do not consider themselves to have that role. *"I'm just one of the ladies"* is often a comment one hears. So a fundamental aspect of development training should be to persuade these wonderful ladies that their role really <u>does</u> have an impact on the task, at unit and departmental level; their team, in terms of it contributing to the success of the school; and also their role in managing individual staff issues.

The real essence of training new team leaders is often to change attitudes: to encourage them to think much more about different customer groups; to encourage them to be more commercially aware; but, most importantly, to stress throughout the training the crucial importance of their leadership role at the task level (unit and departmental) and in terms of developing high performance teams. If successful, the final evaluation sheets should contain a majority view that the training gave them increased confidence and, in particular, a greater feeling of self-worth.

Leadership Mentoring

One of the questions I ask the leaders I interviewed for the Hospitality Leadership Excellence Survey was how they learned their leadership skills. The majority view was that they learned on the job, largely from line managers they had reported to in the past. Most recalled the positive lessons they had learnt, although some mentioned that they learned how <u>not</u> to lead from certain previous managers! There is no doubt that line managers who recognise an important aspect of their role as developing and mentoring their subordinates can have a most powerful influence on them. Mentoring is, however, more than merely good management. It also involves more than merely ensuring that the individual goes on appropriate management and leadership courses. It involves taking a <u>personal</u> responsibility for developing that individual's leadership skills. It also, incidentally, means understanding the importance of one's own example to more junior managers – who will take great benefit from observing your own inspirational leadership.

An open, positive mentoring relationship offers many potential benefits, including:

- Addressing and resolving specific situations associated with the mentee's role.

- Building more constructive relationships within the workplace.

- Clarifying and prioritising work and personal choices.

- Gaining greater confidence and feeling of self worth.

- Improving career development potential and, in particular,

- Developing improved leadership skills founded upon greater confidence in the authority of the mentee's leadership role.

Mentors should use opportunities for delegating tasks and empowering authority to achieve many of the benefits listed above.

A mentoring agreement involves regular meetings, undertaken confidentiality, to discuss progress towards agreed goals, often set at the previous meeting. Such meetings should be used to agree strengths and weaknesses and to discuss means whereby the mentee can address and develop identified leadership shortcomings. Discussion can also surround specific leadership workplace problems that the mentee is experiencing.

Although mentoring is different from formal leadership training, there is a connection in that the mentor should ensure that mentees are well briefed in advance of any such training and understand both the reason they have been sent on it, as well as the expectations placed upon them following its completion. It is important, therefore, that both parties meet shortly after completion of the course to discuss whether the objectives were met. Also, the mentee may have been encouraged and inspired to try out new leadership approaches within the team. A post-training meeting will provide an opportunity to discuss these new approaches and their application with the line manager and to seek appropriate advice and guidance in terms of applying the newly-learnt skills.

Mentoring arrangements, formal or informal, between leaders and their line manager can have very significant benefits in terms of leadership development if they are entered upon enthusiastically and conscientiously by both parties.

A Leadership Development Strategy

The more forward-thinking companies, including those within the HLTT industry whose leaders are showcased in Part II, think hard about ensuring that a strategy exists to create opportunities for employees to map out a career within that particular organisation. One of the leaders I interviewed for my second book, *One Piece Short of a Jigsaw?,* placed great importance on the principle of 'a brightness of future' for his staff. This was a fundamental principle of the company and involved working hard to ensure that employees believed that their futures lay within that company. It required motivating and empowering staff to realise their potential within existing posts and also included serious attention being given to internal career development.

Another, the catering department at the Nottingham University NHS Trust, has what they called 'the skills escalator' as a formal career development policy for their staff. It has five levels, from a pre-employment programme, through to gaining management status. At each level there are individual performance competency reviews and a list of skills, knowledge and development opportunities for that particular grade, in advance of taking the step to the higher grade. This is a very good example of a career development policy that is considered and laid out so that each member of that department understands the necessary steps for their career advancement. The head of department told me that, in his experience, having such a transparent and widely communicated development plan often encouraged otherwise reticent members of staff to work towards promotion.

Another good example of the emphasis placed on career development is found within the Four Seasons hotel group, which operates hotels in a number of countries across the world. It manages a web site whereby job opportunities are promoted in all its hotels. The Regional Vice-President of the group, John Stauss, who is featured in Part II, explained that it is quite normal for members of staff to regularly access the web site with a view to identifying job opportunities elsewhere within the world. Rather than seeing staff moving on as having a negative impact on his particular hotel, he believes that it is his responsibility to encourage staff to better themselves through career development, hopefully within his company. This is not always the case, as leaders sometimes resent staff leaving their organisation to better themselves. The beauty of the Four Seasons system is that it tends to retain quality employees within the group as a whole.

If people are to be groomed for promotion within an organisation it is important that they are given the opportunity to learn, not only the leadership skills required of the next rung on their career ladder, but also a wide range of related skills. More forward-thinking hospitality organisations will move team leaders, for example, between different departments such as reception, restaurant, and accommodation services. Doing so offers many advantages, not least an appreciation of the inter-dependence of different teams in order to deliver the overall task of the operation: providing exceptional customer service. The danger is that employees who are promoted entirely within a single department do not have an appreciation of the bigger picture in terms of the task and the needs of other teams within the company.

Whatever system an organisation has to develop its individuals, it must be recognised as being fair and without favour. The hospitality industry, for example, has a high proportion of female employees in operational roles, especially in the front of house (68 per cent). It is important that organisations recognise the specific demands placed on female employees, many of whom may have other maternal duties, and hence give them every opportunity to realise their potential in terms of career development. Far too many female employees with promotion prospects fall by the wayside due to overly-rigid employment practices – to the disadvantage of our industry and its companies.

Another industry-specific challenge is to ensure that staff that have come to work in the UK from Eastern Europe have an equal opportunity to rise to leadership positions within their work places, as Martina Dudasova has done within Malmaison (Chapter 2.12). Indeed, we have many who are, in fact, over-qualified for the work they initially take up in hospitality. For example, the restaurant chain Nando's Chickenland have taken a high proportion of such workers and have many examples of how their skills have been identified and nurtured to the benefit of the company. One worker, employed in their pan wash area was found to have been a university lecturer in Poland. It is only because Nando's embrace cultural diversity that he was identified and developed to an extent whereby he became a manager of one of their restaurants. Moving from a kitchen porter's role to a significant team leader role required recognition of the importance of career development within the company – one that Nando's, and other hospitality organisations, take very seriously.

How effective is your leadership development strategy?

Most organisations in the UK, certainly the larger ones, will have some form of plan or strategy labelled 'leadership development'. However, in the light of the approach to leadership and its development I have proposed in this book, especially in this chapter, it may be prudent to ask a few searching questions about the current strategy, for example:

- Is it based upon a sound appreciation of what leadership is and how it should be applied? Is it clear exactly what the development initiatives are seeking to develop?

- Does the strategy reflect the fundamental principle that nobody should be given a leadership role without adequate preparation for it?

- How are the resources spread? Are they being lavished on too few people at the top or are the needs of all levels of leadership being addressed?

- Is the strategy being evaluated and, if so, what measurements are used?

- Does the strategy include a system of mentoring whereby line managers are encouraged to guide their junior leaders?

- Are all leaders, or potential leaders, included within the strategy, regardless of gender, ethnicity or nationality?

- Does the selection process adequately identify current and potential leadership skills?

- Does the strategy have the full support of the senior management team, especially the Chief Executive?

This last bullet point is far from the least important – in fact if the top strategic leader is not fully committed to the work of developing leaders, and demonstrates that commitment consistently, the strategy is likely to be doomed from the outset. It is the strategic leadership of an organisation that determines its culture and one that is not based upon principles such as trust, transparency, honesty, integrity and mutual respect will be a hostile environment as far as growing leaders is concerned. If a chief executive does not promote a culture based firmly on these values then the organisation will stunt leaders, rather than nurture and grow them. It is the senior person, sometimes the organisation's founder, who sets the tone and can create an enduring culture that forms the foundation for growth and prosperity. It is fascinating to see how this has happened in the three hotel groups featured in the next chapter on this book.

One way of evaluating the extent to which a development programme is meeting the needs of its participants is to undertake a training needs analysis. Such tools come in a variety of formats but I would like to share with you my company, Hospitality Leadership's, model. It is a questionnaire, completed by individual staff members, that includes the following questions:

1. *Please identify your grade by ticking one of the boxes below* (each grade listed alongside tick-box).

2. *How much training have you had for the job you do now?* (Range from 1, 'none at all', to 10, 'all I need').

3. *How would you rate the quality of training you have had for the job you do now?* (Differentiate between company trainers and external trainers, if appropriate) (Range from 1, 'very poor', to 10, 'excellent').

4. *How much do you agree with the statement: 'I am encouraged to develop my skills and knowledge to the best of my potential'?* (Range from 1, 'strongly disagree', to 10, 'strongly agree')

5. *Are the training opportunities within the organisation well publicised? Are you always aware what training is available to you?* (Range from 1, 'never know what's available' to 10, 'always know what's available').

6. *Do you feel that all your relevant skills are fully used within your current job?* (Yes/No).

7. *If not, please briefly detail below what skills you have that could be better used within your job.* (Space provided to write answer).

8. *What do you think about the current administrative arrangements for training within the organisation? Please indicate any changes you would like to see made in terms of location, timing etc.* (Space provided to write answer).

9. *Do you have sufficient information about your organisation, and the part your team plays in it, if you were asked to explain it to other interested parties?* (Range from 1, 'have no idea about it' to 10, 'fully understand about it').

10. *Please read the management skills listed and numbered on the attached pages* (see Appendix D) *and identify which you are best at; which you need to improve most in; and which you feel are the most important for the future of your team/department/organisation* (use whichever term is most appropriate)*. Identify the skills by putting their number on the lines provided (in any priority order).*

My <u>top ten strengths</u> are:

....

The <u>ten strengths that I need to improve most</u> are:

....

The <u>ten most important skills needed by my
team/department/organisation</u> (delete as appropriate) are:

....

The questionnaires should be completed and returned confidentially. Upon receipt you will be in a position to analyse them to identify both the appropriateness of the current training provision and the areas in need of future development. The last question can be a particularly valuable source of planning data.

In addition to undertaking a training needs analysis, organisations should also evaluate their leadership development strategy, should they have one. Is the organisation getting value for money? Does the strategy deliver the results it intends? Does it provide a common framework to ensure alignment with the corporate vision, values and objectives? Are all aspects of leadership development covered, at all levels?

Two of my fellow Adair Associates, Gordon Watt, a leadership development consultant, and Dr Chris Smewing, an occupational psychologist, have produced a Leadership Development Strategy Audit that is comprised of 48 fundamental statements about leadership strategy, grouped under the following ten headings:

- Strategic purpose
- Strategy
- Sponsorship
- Organisational structure and culture
- Planning
- Roles
- Direction and personal objectives
- Selection and assignment
- Training and development
- Assessment

It is an on-line questionnaire, designed for chief executives and HR directors, which results in a report that identifies both the strengths of their leadership development strategy and potential areas for improvement. Most who have completed the audit report that it offered insights which they immediately recognised, but had never previously appreciated.

If you would like to find out more you can take a **free trial** at www.adairleadershipdevelopment.co.uk/audit.html. The trial only takes 10-15 minutes and results in a report for you to assess the likely value of the full audit.

As a conclusion to this chapter, here is a quick checklist for organisation intent on growing their own leaders:

- Select good seeds – choose people who display the generic qualities of good leadership.

- Prepare the soil – does the organisation's culture and policies feed or stunt leadership growth?

- <u>Fertilise and water</u> – invest in your people. Continually reinforce values such as honesty, integrity, trust, mutual respect.

- <u>Apply weed killer</u> – to those negative influences that stifle growth.

- <u>Rotate the crops</u> – give leaders a variety of challenges and opportunities.

- <u>Let the fields lie fallow</u> – give leaders time to think, experiment, make mistakes – in order to benefit from those experiences.

- <u>Transplant, as necessary</u> - a leader who struggles in one field may thrive in another.

- <u>Prune the dead wood</u> – abandon practices that do not work and say farewell to those employees who do not subscribe to and practice the organisation's values.

- <u>Display the fruits</u> – celebrate the success of the leadership development strategy. Use its champions to motivate others to join.

- <u>Harvest the benefits</u> – in terms of employee commitment, customer satisfaction, and bottom-line profits.

1.6 THE ENDURING CULTURE OF HOTEL FOUNDERS

During my research for this book, in particular the interviews with the leadership champions for Part II, it became apparent to me that, in some companies in particular, a deeply-embedded culture exists that underpins so much of their approach to their customers and, especially, their staff.   The Oxford English Dictionary defines culture as *'the customs, institutions and achievements of a particular nation, people or group'*.   The culture of any organisation is the combined product of the beliefs, values and attitudes of all those who belong to it, or work within it.   But how are those beliefs, values and attitudes formed and subsequently influenced?   Very often they were formed at the organisation's conception by its founder, who had both deeply held beliefs, and the courage and conviction to cement them as the foundation upon which to build the business.   Indeed, sometimes those beliefs, values and attitudes were contrary to the prevailing thinking of business and society at that time.

Take Anita Roddick as an example: she built Body Shop into an internationally successful operation that not only created a strong and loyal customer base, but also played a major role in influencing society's views on a range of ethical trading issues.   For her, Body Shop was much more than an outlet for environmentally friendly cosmetics; it was a flagship for a new way of thinking.   As she explained, *"I want to work for a company that contributes to, and is part of, the community. I want something not just to invest in. I want something to believe in".*

In terms of leadership, for me there is no greater modern-day example of someone who introduced a dramatically new way of thinking than Ricardo Semler. In 1982 he took over his father's company, Semco, that manufactured industrial pumps in Brazil – one he described as *"a traditional company in every respect, with a pyramidal structure and a rule for every contingency"* – and tore up the rule book. As The Times describes, 'Semco takes workplace democracy to previously unimagined frontiers', in that:

- Workers make the decisions previously made by the bosses.

- Managerial staff set their own salaries and bonuses.

- Shop floor workers set their own productivity targets and schedules.

- Everyone has access to the company books and accounts.

Revolutionary it may be, but it has certainly proved successful: increasing Semco's turnover from $4m in 1982 to $212m in 2003, and becoming one of Latin America's fastest-growing companies and one with a waiting list of thousands of applicants hoping to join it. Its success is a result of an empowerment culture based upon Semler's unshakable belief in his staff and their potential. *"If we do not allow people to do things the way they do, we will never know what they are capable of and they will just follow our boarding school rules."*

I believe his book *'Maverick'* should be required reading for every leadership course for middle or senior managers – it is on the ones my company runs!

Ricardo Semler is certainly a fine example of a leader who built a business based upon his own deep-rooted convictions; as is Anita Roddick, who also founded and developed hers on a culture predicated upon her own personal beliefs. Sometimes the influence of a company's founder can extend over decades, even through generations, and there are good examples of this within our own hospitality industry- as became apparent during my interviews with leaders from three companies, in particular. Personally, I find that the stories of how their founders built an enduring company culture that continues to direct every facet of its operation provide a fascinating and illuminating lesson on leadership that I would like to share with you.

J Willard Marriott

The $3 billion hotel empire that now has 3,000 hotels, employing 169,000 people in 69 countries, certainly had humble beginnings. It all started in 1927, when J Willard 'Bill' Marriott and his, newly married, wife Alice opened a root beer stand in Washington DC. During his last year of college in Salt Lake City, an A & W root beer stand had opened near the University of Utah campus and Bill had been impressed with how rapidly it had drawn in customers. Hence, soon after, having moved to Washington, they bought an A & W franchise for $6,000 and opened their own stand, quickly building a loyal customer base and subsequently adding additional outlets. However, they quickly realised that, whilst their drinks sold well during the hot summer months, business was not so good during winter so they added barbecued beef sandwiches and tacos to the menu and renamed their restaurant Hot Shoppe.

By 1932, Hot Shoppes had evolved into a chain of restaurants along the highways from New York to Florida. One day, Bill noticed people buying food from the Washington Hot Shoppe and carrying it to the local airport to eat whilst on board an aircraft. From this observation, he launched a new service that provided boxed lunches to airlines, named In-Flite, which would eventually become the world's largest airline catering business. In 1957, Marriott opened its first hotel, the Twin Bridges Motor Hotel, in Arlington, Virginia, near both the Pentagon and Washington National Airport. From there, over the years, Marriott has moved into a range of other hospitality ventures from theme parks to cruise ships; creating what, President Ronald Reagan described as *"a living example of the American Dream"*.

From his earliest ventures, Bill Marriott built his business on one simple concept – that caring for his staff, or associates as he called them, and giving them an opportunity to contribute, was the formula for success. As he said, *"Take care of Marriott people and they will take care of Marriott guests"*. Being somewhat of an extrovert, he was never happier than when surrounded by his people and engaged in a lively conversation or friendly debate. Marriott's corporate history is full of stories of Bill, perched comfortably on a hotel lobby sofa, listening to the family problems of one of his associates, while the hotel's senior managers cooled their heels waiting for him to return to the office. He felt strongly that the concerns and problems of the people who worked for him should always be listened to as, in his eyes, a successful company puts its employees first. Throughout his life he never missed an opportunity to reinforce his belief in the fundamental importance of cared-for, motivated staff to the success of his business empire, often saying to his managers *"I get a lot of letters from our customers. They don't tell us how beautiful our ballroom was, they tell us how wonderful our people were"*.

In 1932, whilst Bill and Alice Marriott were building up their Hot Shoppe business, their first son, J Willard Jnr, was born. At the age of 14 years Bill Jnr took his first job with the company, stapling invoices in the accounting department, and continued thereon to learn every aspect of the restaurant business, gradually taking on more managerial responsibilities. Indeed, it was he who persuaded his father to raise the money in order to branch out into hotels in the

1950s. In 1963 Bill Snr turned over the presidency of his growing company to his eldest son, although remaining actively involved as CEO until his death in 1985.

Bill Marriott Jnr now continues the legacy of his father, in particular the people-centred culture which he describes as *"The life-thread and glue that links our past, present and future"*. In his book, *The Spirit to Serve*, he argues that putting employees first is particularly important to Marriott because it operates in the people business, not just the service business. His associates supply their customers with the answers to two of life's basic needs – food and accommodation; and are therefore touching on special human territory. The customers, whether they are conscious of it or not, have definite expectations about not only the tangible aspects of eating and sleeping – good food, a comfortable bed – but also the intangibles of those experiences – how they are greeted; how their questions are answered; how their special problems are handled. That is where, he contends, the human touch can make the difference between a mediocre or poor experience and a positive, even unforgettable, one. Yet, if the people who are responsible for supplying that human interaction are unhappy, tired, poorly trained, or otherwise demotivated, they are not going to impact positively on the guest experience.

During Bill Marriott Snr's tenure of the company, a set of core values were conceived that continue to form the cornerstone of the company's *Spirit to Serve* philosophy. In relation to associates, these include:

- The unshakeable conviction that our people are our most important asset.

- An environment that supports associate growth and personal development.

- A reputation for employing caring, dependable associates who are ethical and trustworthy.

- A performance-reward system that recognises the important contributions of both hourly and management associates.

- Pride in the Marriott name, accomplishments, and record of success.

- A home-like atmosphere and friendly workplace relationships.

- A hands-on management style ie 'management by walking around'.

- Openness to innovation and creativity in serving guests.

One hears so many strategic leaders say 'our people are our most important asset' that it is easy to become cynical, especially when the organisations they represent often fall well short of living that ideal in their daily dealings with their staff and their customers. Equally, it is fashionable today for businesses to talk about themselves as 'families'. However, during my interviews with Marriott leaders, some of whom like Gary Dodds, are included in Part II, I became convinced that the company's core values do, indeed, influence the beliefs, values and attitudes of those whose responsibility it is to perpetuate the cultural legacy of its founder, J Willard Marriott Snr002E

Isadore Sharp

Warren Bennis, Professor of Business at the University of Southern California and oft-quoted authority on management and leadership, has said of Isadore Sharpe

"This isn't just another rags-to-riches story but a story about a leader who embodies three essential qualities of exemplary leadership – trust, integrity, and optimism – and how he leveraged those values to create quality at Four Seasons, and how just about every business that cares about excellence can do the same."

Isadore Sharpe's entry into the hospitality industry is not too dissimilar to Bill Marriott Snr's and its outcome is also very similar – the creation of a large, highly respected, international hotel group. Yet, in 1961 when he built his first hotel he knew nothing about the business. He was the son of a Polish Jew who had earlier played his part in developing the desert area that was to become the State of Israel. His mother's oldest brother, Max, emigrated to Canada, paying his way by working on ships and ending up by chance in Toronto, where he prospered and gradually brought over his extended family, one by one. So it was that Isadore's father moved from Israel to Toronto, married in 1927, and fathered four children, one of them Isadore in 1931.

His father worked through the Great Depression, taking jobs anywhere he could get them, until he had learned enough to become a plastering contractor. His English was, however, a problem for him, especially in terms of tendering for contracts. On one occasion he misread the specification for a job, which resulted in him entering a quote that was only half what it should have been, given the extent of the work involved. Not surprisingly, his bid was readily accepted but he did not realise his mistake until he was well into the job. However, having made a commitment he felt honour-bound to keep it so he finished the contract without compromising quality, even though it meant him working for several years to pay off the resulting debt. Isadore, his son, was only told the story later but it became a lesson in business ethics that he has remembered throughout his life.

His father developed his business strategy whereby he would buy a piece of land and build a house upon it, in which his family lived whilst he was building another. Hence, by his mid-teens Isadore had moved some fifteen times which, he now believes, made him independent at a very early age. He also spent a good deal of his time helping his father, thus construction became very much a part of his life – to such an extent that he went to Ryerson Polytechnic School, now a university, to study architecture, graduating at twenty-one years of age. He immediately joined his father and, in time, took over the business, which flourished in a city, Toronto, which was growing rapidly into both a cosmopolitan and a financial centre. It was while he was negotiating a loan from his bank that the manager gave him some advice, *"Why don't you get rid of the rubber boots and start working with pencil and paper instead of pick and shovel?"*. He was suggesting that Isadore had a good business mind and should use it to build the business, rather than personally building apartments.

Yet it was not until his honeymoon, two or three years later, that he began to think in business terms. The airport hotel they stayed in was a successful operation, yet the facilities were anything but glamorous. Isadore began to think that if a hotel like that was making lots of money, it shouldn't be hard to build another that would make even more. Around that time a friend of his had asked him to build a modest motel with just seven rooms on either side of a central office and storage room, close to a junction of Highway 27. Isadore suggested extending the roof so that it would house a huge sign – MOTEL 27 – whilst offering the capability of adding further rooms at a later date.

The idea worked, extra rooms were added, and the motel was a great success; encouraging him to think 'If it works so well here, why wouldn't it work downtown?'. Thus the germ of an idea was born that would result in the first Four Seasons hotel being built at the junction of Jarvis Street and Carlton, Toronto in 1961: the first of what would become one of the largest and most prestigious group of five-star hotels in the world.

In his recent book, *Four Seasons – The Story of a Business Philosophy*, Isadore Sharp ends its introduction thus:

> *"Over the years, we've initiated many new ideas that have been copied and are now the norm in the industry. But the one idea that our customers value the most cannot be copied: the consistent quality of our exceptional service. That service is based upon a corporate culture, and a culture cannot be mandated as a policy. It must grow from within, based upon the actions of the company's people over a long period of time. Four Seasons is the sum of its people – many, many good people."*

What an interesting set of observations: exceptional service is based upon a corporate culture; a culture cannot be mandated as a policy; it must grow from within, based upon the continuing actions of the company's people. He goes further in his book to explain how, in Four Seasons' formative years, he had to convince his senior management team that the company's future success had to be based upon a culture of exceptional customer service – provided by staff who were given the opportunity to do just that.

For him, it was all about treating employees the way they are expected to treat their customers: with the same care and understanding. The concept was embodied in an expression he had previously heard, 'We are only what we do, not what we say we are'. Not too dissimilar from 'Actions speak louder than words', perhaps. However, it was difficult to change the attitudes of his managers who, like most at that time, believed that employee performance was to be guaranteed only by close supervision and the application of a detailed set of rules and regulations. Most managers at that time had been trained to assume that employees did not work harder than they had to, hence they had to be driven by the stick, rather than enticed by the carrot. What Isadore was proposing was a complete turnaround in attitude, theory and practice. It was, indeed, revolutionary thinking for the mid-1970s, although not so for the twenty-first century leader, I hope!

Not only did he have to get his senior management on board, but he then had to distil this new thinking throughout all his hotels. For most of his hotel general managers and their management teams it was not so much a process of learning new leadership techniques, as unlearning previously held management theory. Teamwork may have been a word commonly used, but actually what it involved was groups of people who did what they were told, referring any problems to their managers. Isadore envisaged a workforce that willingly and immediately solved any service-related problems as they arose. Only by doing so, could his vision of a consistent quality of exceptional service be realised.

Ask anyone in a leadership position: changing people's attitudes is one of the greatest challenges of a leader. That is why John Stauss, who features in Part II of this book, explained in my interview with him that it was Four Seasons' policy to recruit people with a positive attitude, who can then be trained in the skills and knowledge necessary for their jobs. So it was that Isadore Sharp spent several of the early years touring hotels telling management at every level that they cannot change their employees' behaviour unless they changed their own. He wanted front-line staff who thought for themselves and acted to remedy service failures on the spot: seeing the company's interests as their own and voluntarily taking personal responsibility for service delivery within their workplace. In effect, to become self-managers. His message to the managers was therefore, *'Keep your egos in check and let the people who work for you shine, because they're the people who know our customers best. They are the people we depend on to lead the way. It's no longer 'Do as I say'. It's now 'Do as I do.''* It was an uphill struggle as some GMs didn't want to empower subordinates who may become rivals, whilst others still saw employees as a cost, rather than a benefit. For some it was still 'us and them', rather than merely 'us'.

For years, he struggled to change hearts and minds until, in 1980, he decided that he could no longer tolerate the remaining managers who were still not prepared to act as role models for the empowerment culture he espoused. He realised that he needed a written code of values that would bring all his people together under one Golden Rule, namely 'Do unto others as you would have them do unto you'. The idea was discussed, staff at all levels within the hotels were consulted, and finally the Golden Rule was accepted as Four Seasons' company touchstone; which has subsequently been developed into its current 'Statement of Our Goals, Our Beliefs, Our Principles':

WHO WE ARE

We have chosen to specialise within the hospitality industry by offering only experiences of exceptional quality. Our objective is to be recognised as the company that manages the finest hotels, resorts and residence clubs wherever they are located. We create properties of enduring value using superior design and finishes, and we support them with a deeply instilled ethic of personal service. Doing so allows Four Seasons to satisfy the needs and tastes of our discriminating customers and to maintain our position as the world's premier hospitality company.

HOW WE BEHAVE

We demonstrate our beliefs most meaningfully in the way we treat each other and by the example we set for one another. In all our interactions with our guests, customers, business associates, and colleagues, we seek to deal with others as we would have them deal with us.

WHAT WE BELIEVE

Our greatest asset, and the key to our success, is our people. We believe that each of us needs a sense of dignity, pride and satisfaction in what we do. Because satisfying our guests depends on the united efforts of many, we are most effective when we work together cooperatively, respecting each other's contributions and importance.

HOW WE SUCCEED

We succeed when every decision is based on a clear understanding of and belief in what we do and when we couple this conviction with sound financial planning. We expect to achieve a fair and reasonable profit to ensure the prosperity of the company and to offer long-term benefits to our customers, our employees, our hotel owners, and our shareholders.

In more recent years, when Isadore speaks to his people about the Four Seasons' culture and the Golden Rule that underpins it he relates it to the way they bring up their own children – with certain principles, values and work ethics. Whilst his staff may well be diverse in terms of age, gender, backgrounds, beliefs etc, the tie that binds them together is their value system – the principles they believe in and which makes the company homogeneous.

In his crusading years, before the culture was embedded within his company, there were some managers who remained unconvinced of the business benefits of divesting their staff of the chains of managerial control. It is true, as always, that not everyone is prepared to change deeply-held attitudes and so some of the more intransigent managers had to be released and more open-minded replacements recruited. Change can only happen if those in senior positions embrace it and lead by example. Its Founder was resolute that business success would only be achieved in the luxury hotel sector Four Seasons was seeking to establish itself in if staff were inspired by their leaders to do everything in their power to provide exceptional customer service.

A marvellous example of exactly that happened in 1989, six months after the Chicago Four Seasons Hotel opened and it was hosting a small fund-raising event for sixty people, fronted by President and Nancy Reagan. Every gentleman wore a black tie, except one who was heard speaking to his wife as donors lined up to have their pictures taken with the former President and First Lady. *"You could have told me that it was black tie. If you had, I wouldn't feel such an idiot!"*. His whispered comments were heard by an employee, Hans Willimann, who invited the guest to follow him to the uniform office where the manager there changed out of the tuxedo he was wearing and put on his civilian clothes. He then dashed into the laundry to press his tuxedo for the guest to wear. The trousers were a little too big so the staff seamstress made a hasty adjustment before the gentleman rejoined the party.

The next day Hans received a lengthy and effusive letter of praise from the guest, who turned out to be the Chairman and CEO of the global consulting firm, A T Kearney. In it he suggested that, were his consultants to have the kind of attitude that Hans and his colleagues had demonstrated, the company could be twice its size.

From that time forward, all of A T Kearney's functions have been held in Four Seasons Hotels, resulting in millions of dollars revenue. And at every one, that once-under-dressed gentleman would rise and recount his story so that his colleagues would never forget where the bar was to be set in terms of exceeding customer expectations.

Hans Willimann is a prime example of how a culture such as that within Four Seasons can have a powerful effect in a multitude of ways. He says openly, having worked for thirty years with the company, that its philosophy has changed him as a person and has inspired him to raise his own children with a hands-off approach.

When people are trusted and respected they are more likely to demonstrate trust and respect in return. Hence, for leaders who want to create a culture based upon openness, transparency, trust and mutual respect they could do worse than adopting the Golden Rule Isadore Sharp founded his hotel group upon and which endures to this day – 'Do unto others as you would have them do unto you'.

Jasminder Singh

I was making a presentation to the managers of the Radisson Edwardian hotel group a couple of years ago. I asked them to shout the brand values of some well known companies. Firstly, I said "Marks and Spencer" and several of the group shouted back "quality". I then said "Body Shop" and got replies such as "environmentally friendly" and "not tested on animals". I then said 'Radisson Edwardian Hotels' and, almost without exception, the audience returned "Making People Feel Special".

It was a dramatic example of a group of employees who had embraced the values of their company – as conceived by its founder, Jasminder Singh. I tried the same exercise with the management team of another prestigious five-star hotel shortly after and their responses to the two high street retailers were the same but when I then shouted the name of their own hotel there was silence – yet, like Radisson Edwardian Hotels, the group to which this hotel belongs also has a strap line representing the quality values it aspires to. To me, the different reaction of the two groups of managers demonstrated how some organisations have been able to engage their employees to buy into a set of cultural values, whilst others have not.

Jasminder Singh founded the Edwardian Group in 1977 and joined with Radisson, part of Carlson Hotels Worldwide, in 1993. He had come to the UK from Nairobi in 1970 as an eighteen-year old and qualified as an accountant six years later. Jasminder conceived and commenced a strategy of buying run-down hotels and upgrading them to the highest standards. His business model was to create standards of comfort that were not common in those days, and then to sell the rooms at competitive rates, thus maximising occupancy.

When interviewed for an article in the magazine *Catering Times* in 1984, Jasminder explained that he worked hard to achieve a family atmosphere within his hotel teams so that his people felt a part of the company, rather than just a number. His business at that time was expanding rapidly and he needed a professional team within it – one with high standards that complemented the quality philosophy he was promoting. He was competing against Grand Metropolitan and Forte for the best industry staff so he had to offer something different to entice the talent he sought.

His employment offer involved inviting people to share his passion for excellence and then giving them opportunities to develop within his young, but rapidly growing, company. Training was then, and still is, something that Radisson Edwardian takes seriously and is prepared to allocate resources to. Moreover, their training programmes include designated leadership development – from the 'Future Leaders Programme' for team leaders; to their strategic leaders attending leadership courses at Oxford Saïd Business School. Jasminder has also formally endorsed Hospitality Leadership's *Certificate in Team Leadership* training course (Appendix C). Personally, I am not aware of another hospitality organisation of similar size that is so focused on the leadership development of its people.

One of the foundations of their employment policy is full staff empowerment: balancing an expectation of responsibility with an equal measure of autonomy to ensure that hotel guests enjoy better levels of service and faster solutions to any problems they encounter. To achieve the level of guest satisfaction necessary to meet their very demanding occupancy targets, they recognise the need for a strong, clear set of customer service values which include:

- Making people feel special. Paying special attention to guests and understanding them so well that their needs are anticipated and delivered even before they have to ask. To do so, however, requires staff who buy into and deliver that vision; which, judging by their reaction to my brand values exercise, has been achieved.

- Luxury without pretension. Jasminder Singh is, himself, a modest man who shuns the publicity that could accompany the Chairman and CEO of a successful company. I believe that his low-key persona, coupled with his passionate belief in the highest possible standards of service, has fundamentally determined the style of his hotels. Such is Jasminder's personality: understated yet passionate, especially in terms of service delivery, and certainly not pretentious.

I sometimes think that there is a danger when hospitality organisations are run by accountants, rather than caterers, that controls and processes are introduced that strangle creative thinking. Moreover, as companies get bigger their strategic leaders run the risk of becoming ever more distant from the front line. Sophisticated tools are introduced to control the business, along with a range of key performance indicators, which can encourage a clinical approach to service delivery, stifling initiative and calculated risk taking.

Indeed, in mid-2008 Jasminder began to wonder if the connection between the company and its people had begun to unravel. It has always been his objective to encourage an emotional engagement and loyalty from his staff; in exchange for the employment and career opportunities offered to them. Even from his early days, he had sought to encourage an open, transparent environment where information was shared and upward communication encouraged. He, himself, had led by example in this respect by visiting each of his central London hotels every morning before going to his office. But pressure of work had meant that he was doing his rounds less and less. He was meeting his senior people just as often, but was not finding the time to speak to, and listen to, those at the sharp end so much as before.

About that time, the company experienced some bad media publicity, suggesting poor staff practices, which caused Jasminder to question whether standards of leadership at all levels within the hotels were as strong as they had previously been. Hence, he instigated a programme of communication that involved him personally meeting staff at all levels in order to better understand what obstacles had been created that were driving a wedge between the organisation and its most important people – those who served the guests. He found a workforce that were not as willing as before to take the initiative; less prepared to challenge the rules and process that were inhibiting their ability to 'make people feel special'.

Jasminder had perhaps allowed the culture he had built his company upon to become less people-focused and more process-driven. He had always encouraged his people to, as he described it to me, 'bring their magic with them'. Surely, the message for us is, therefore, that for the founder to build a business upon a profoundly-held set of beliefs that underpin its culture he or she must never allow those founding principles to become diluted.

They must be embedded so deeply within the organisation, and practiced so demonstratively and consistently by the founder and every leader at every level, as to be the very life force upon which the organisation exists and prospers. The culture must, indeed, be enduring.

PART II

LEADERSHIP CHAMPIONS

INTRODUCTION

"If your actions inspire others to dream more; learn more; do more; and become more – you are a leader"

John Quincy Adams

US President, 1825 – 1829

In writing this book, I not only wanted to explain my approach to leadership within my industry, and what I have learnt from working a lifetime within it, but also to showcase the example shown by others who have demonstrated through their actions and attitude how powerful inspirational leadership can be. But how to find such people from within the approximately two million people employed within the hospitality, leisure, tourism and travel industry?

To do so, as with the Hospitality Leadership Excellence Survey (Appendix B), I directed my attention towards the organisations that have been recognised as good employers through the Sunday Times '100 Best Companies to Work For' and/or the Caterer and Hotelkeeper magazine's 'Best Places to Work in Hospitality' Awards. The table at the end of this introduction lists those featured in the Sunday Times survey since 2004 and that of the Caterer and Hotelkeeper since it introduced the awards in 2006.

With the support of People 1st, I approached all those organisations recognised up to, and including, 2008 (the 2009 winners had not been announced at that time) and invited them to nominate one, or more, team, operational or strategic leaders who they felt were especially worthy of recognition for their exceptional leadership skills. It could have been, for example, that they had:

- Faced and overcome unusual challenges at work
- Developed and inspired high-performing teams
- Applied exceptional leadership skills to lead their team to achieve business success
- Displayed inspirational example to colleagues and staff
- Raised standards of service delivery through sheer determination and strength of character

In the event, ten organisations put forward a total of 28 nominees, of whom I interviewed 21 over the period May 2009 to January 2010. All were great leaders – a credit to their organisations and their industry – but some had a unique story to tell and it is those that are included, with their agreement, in the following chapters.

During the meetings I sought to explore their approach to, and experience of, leadership in the context of their own roles and responsibilities. What special challenges had they faced and overcome? How did they go about inspiring their people to provide exceptional service? How had they learnt their leadership skills? What motivates them as leaders? What do they think makes a great leader? Are there any special leadership challenges within the industry and sector in which they work?

Finally, I asked them 'The $64,000 Question':

> *"If you had to give one piece of advice to someone entering the hospitality industry as a leader with similar responsibilities as yourself, what would it be?*

How fascinating it was to hear their views: all of which were as different as they were insightful – true pearls of wisdom! Current and prospective leaders within our industry, and elsewhere, who 'aspire to inspire' would do well to read the responses listed at Appendix E and consider how to apply them in their own working environments.

Interviewing these leadership champions was not only a great pleasure for me, but it was also a true learning experience. Nobody is too old to learn and I certainly benefited a great deal from hearing from those who are actually applying inspirational leadership within our industry. It is both motivating and encouraging to be in the presence of such passionately driven people. I hope my readers gain as much from reading their stories as I did from recording them.

My sincere thanks go to all those organisations that supported me in this aspect of the book: those who nominated their staff and, especially, those leaders who spared the time to meet me, whether their stories ultimately featured in the book or not.

Table – Hospitality Companies Featuring in The Sunday Times '100 Best Companies to Work For' and the Caterer and Hotelkeeper magazine's 'Best Places to Work in Hospitality' Awards, 2004 – 2009

	SUNDAY TIMES	THE 'CATERER'
ABode Hotels		2009
Aramark (Catering Alliance)	2004	
Bartlett Mitchell		2008
Baxter Storey (Holroyd Howe)	2005, 2006	
Bettys & Taylors	2004, 2005, 2006, 2007	2006
Botanic Inns	2005, 2007, 2009	2007
Bourne Leisure	2008, 2009	
Brookwood Partnership	2008	2006, 2007, 2009

Compass	2005	
Connect Catering		2009
Ego Restaurants		2007
Four Seasons Hotels		2006, 2008
Gala Coral (Gala Bingo)	2006, 2007	
Hayley Conference Centres	2006	
ICC group/NEC		2007
InterContinental London		2009
Inventive Leisure	2008	
La Tasca Restaurants		2006
Lexington Catering	2009	
Malmaison Hotel du Vin		2007, 2008
Mandarin Oriental Hotel	2007	
Marriott Hotels	2008, 2009	
McDonalds Restaurants		2007, 2008, 2009
Nandos Chickenland	2005	
Nottingham University NHS Trust		2006
Q Hotels		2009
Radisson Edwardian Hotels		2006
Ragdale Hall	2005	
Red Carnation Hotels		2009
Starwood Hotels	2008	2007
The Dorchester		2008
The Peach Pub Company		2008, 2009
Whitbread (incl Travel Inns in 04)	2004, 2007	

<u>2.1 JAMES HORLER</u>

Executive Chairman, Ego Restaurants

FROM HUMBLE BEGINNING

Many of us can claim to have started out in the hospitality industry by working in hotels from an early age – but few have crafted such successful careers from such lowly beginnings as James Horler, Executive Chairman of Ego Restaurants.

It was in 1981 when, as a 16 year old, James was contemplating what he wanted to do with the rest of his life. He had a few O Levels but no interest in pursuing any further academic qualifications. His main love was sport, but damaged leg ligaments put paid to any aspirations in that direction, so he listed on a single sheet of paper all the opportunities that may be open to him; a list that included the hotel industry. Despite there being no family connection whatsoever, he decided that he would have a go at hotel and catering management. The plan was to apply for an Ordinary National Diploma in Hotel Management, commencing in the September, before which he would gain some industry experience.

Perhaps as a first sign of his future 'can do' attitude, he wrote to all the hotels in Cambridge, his home town, offering to work for the summer season, without pay – an offer that was readily taken up by the city's Trust House Forte hotel. So was James's sparkling career in the hospitality industry born – washing up pots and pans for nothing for THF! However, his initiative had not gone unnoticed and it was not long before he was offered a place on the in-house management development programme of Family Brand Hotels, a division of THF, which he agreed to, rather than taking up the OND he had previously planned. There cannot be many as successful leaders within the hospitality industry whose qualifications are limited to a handful of 'O' levels, but James Horler had found his vocation and was determined to reap the rewards it offers.

There followed a period as a night manager in a group of hotels in The Lakes; conference and banqueting manager at Ascot; and an appointment at the Swindon Post House. James was still little more than 20 years old when, in 1985, he accepted a post as a unit manager for Little Chef. During his time with the company he enjoyed a meteoric rise to Regional Director by the age of 25, before he was approached by Granada Hospitality. He spent three years with Granada, having responsibility for a £270m budget, when he began to get itchy feet. He was looking for a different challenge and decided to move sideways to a small business with only two restaurants, called Frankie and Benny's. Perhaps it was here that James became a true entrepreneur. Having developed the brand concept from Diner to New York Italian Restaurant and Bar, with 65 outlets across the country, he raised sufficient funds to propose a management buy-out from the parent company, City Centre Restaurants (now The Restaurant Group). However, a new Chief Executive decided not to close the deal – a decision James now recognises to have been a shrewd decision.

Despite this disappointment, James was not to be deterred – he had got the appetite to forge his own path in business. Another opportunity arose in 2001 and he raised £28m to buy La Tasca, a group of 16 tapas restaurants.

What makes a successful entrepreneur? Many will say that it is a combination of fierce determination; vision to see an opportunity and the courage to make it happen; and, perhaps at times, a liberal dose of luck. It certainly seems that all factors came into play with the purchase of La Tasca. Negotiations were completed with contracts signed at 2.00 am on 11 September 2001. James resigned from City Centre Restaurants later that morning and travelled to Manchester to meet with the La Tasca management team and explain his vision for the future of the company. Shortly after the meeting ended, the planes flew into the Twin Towers and La Tasca experienced the worst trading day in its history, with several equally scary weeks to follow! The banks began to get cold feet as the company strove to meet its loan repayment responsibilities and were seeking repayment of their investment.

Hearing this story, one may be excused for thinking that James's luck as an entrepreneur had deserted him. However, as he explains, the deal would never have happened had its completion been scheduled for a mere few hours later and he would never have had the opportunity to develop the business. And develop it he certainly did: expanding to 74 restaurants, floating it for £54m in 2005 and selling it for £130m in 2007. There cannot be many other business enterprises where success has been determined by the passage of so few hours! James looks back at his time with La Tasca with intense satisfaction, especially as every stakeholder in the business, from its employees to the private equity funders, benefited financially from it.

With money in the bank, James and his management team decided to take some time off. However, the time came when the entrepreneurial juices began to flow again and he bought a small group of four outlets – Ego Restaurants. It was interesting to me that, during the interview, James continually used the word "we" when describing his business deals. It is symptomatic of the loyalty he engenders in those around him that his executive management team have followed him through his various career moves: his Commercial Director since Granada Hospitality; his Property Director since Frankie and Benny's; and his Finance Director since La Tasca.

For me, James's leadership style was illuminating, especially for such a high-profile, successful hospitality entrepreneur. He has never lost the human touch; revelling in how he can provide opportunities for his staff to develop. When I asked him what motivates him most, he replied without hesitation *"Seeing my people progress within the company"*. He certainly enjoys building brands, but it is the people that give him most satisfaction. He describes his business philosophy as 'Think Big. Act Small'. 'Think Big' – he wants to create a growing business that people can grow within. 'Act Small' – never lose sight of the little things that matter: being approachable and recognising the crucial importance of every team member. He stresses that he would not want to grow a company to such an extent that he was not able to keep in contact with every restaurant, every member of staff. The company has no head office for its executives to hide in; only a finance office for its Finance Director and three clerks. Other senior managers work independently and are expected to spend most of their time visiting the restaurants. James, himself, visits every one of the nine at least once a week, often managing four visits a day.

I asked him how he would describe the culture of Ego Restaurants and he answered:

"The culture is open. The culture is honest. The culture is integrity. The culture is delivering what is expected. The culture is reward. The culture is ambition. The culture is drive. The culture is development. The culture is open communications. We have nothing to hide."

Whilst the company expects its unit managers to meet challenging financial targets, it is prepared to leave them, with support, to get on with delivering them. Using a footballing analogy, James explains that he expects his managers to be 'Premier League Players', who can stand on their own feet and make their own decisions. Championship managers will not last long with Ego Restaurants. As far as James is concerned, budgets are about banking and are for the Finance Director to worry about; whilst restaurants are about customers spending money, who are the responsibility of the restaurant managers. Moreover, things can change quickly in the restaurant business, so profit targets are set for unit managers no further ahead than one month.

James is a restaurateur through and through and revels in being involved in the day-to-day operation. Previous to our discussion, one of his restaurant managers was on holiday when it had a function for 150 Rotarians so James took over and ran it – and loved the experience. He would not want to lead a restaurant group that was too large for him to be involved with its customers. Indeed, our meeting was interrupted on several occasions as James jumped up to open the restaurant door for a customer, or to offer assistance to another who wanted to pay his bill!

There is no question that James fulfils the role of a strategic leader with distinction, yet he never loses sight of the little things that matter. He knows precisely where he wants Ego to be in three years and sees his role as putting in place a solid platform upon which his staff can build the business. He continually asks himself whether what he does contributes to the bigger plan. Does he understand his people enough? Are they fired up enough in order to ensure that the day-to-day delivery of product and service is contributing to his vision of having 25-30 restaurants in three years time?

Developing the business depends heavily upon building the brand, something that James excels in. Yet he is determined that he should not be seen as the brand as, perhaps, Richard Branson is to Virgin. He would be concerned if he felt that a company was totally dependent upon his personal leadership. For him, success is growing a business on such a sound foundation that it will continue to develop once he has moved on. Indeed, he is very proud that Frankie and Benny's, that had 65 outlets when he left, now boasts 140.

He believes that businesses grow in cycles and require different leadership at different times and that his strength lies in developing fledgling enterprises to a size whereby he can still apply the personal touch. His role is to create a business where sound structures are in place and where its people are developed and motivated to drive it forward. As he says, *"I may have my hand on the tiller, but I do not have to put wind in the sails"*.

It was fascinating talking to someone with such a deep understanding of the restaurant sector of the hospitality industry, especially during such challenging, recessionary times. He explained to me that, over recent months, customer expectations had changed significantly. At all levels of spending, customers are becoming increasingly price-conscious and are looking for better value from restaurant operators. Ego is now getting people booking tables for eight and asking for a discount – that would never have happened even six months previously.

James believes that the recession has forced casual dining restaurants to split along two lines. Firstly, there are the bigger companies that dominate the market, but often have to service significant loan repayments. Turnover is critical to these players so they have taken the route of heavy discounting – two-for-one deals for example. However, they are big enough to do so whilst maintaining their profit levels. Then there are the smaller players, like Ego Restaurants, with no debt but with much less critical mass within the market. They cannot pressurise suppliers as much as the big chains, so they are having to think smarter about their offering in order to compete in the increasingly price-conscious market. For example, James recognised that Ego's pricing may soon be regarded as being in the upper limits for casual diners so he was working with his chefs to offer cheaper menu choices, but with carefully controlled food costs so as to maintain gross profit margins, whilst ensuring that quality is improved.

Looking ahead, James believes, as the grip of the recessions loosens, the bigger players will struggle to withdraw their discounted offers as customer expectations will have been firmly established. For restaurant groups like Ego, it will the responsibility of strategic leaders to find ways to reposition their offer in order for customers to perceive it as being better value than cheaper, discounted deals.

They will then have to empower and motivate their teams to ensure that this strategy bears fruit.

For me, I have no doubt that that is precisely what James Horler will do!

2.2 JOHN STAUSS

Regional Vice President,
Four Seasons Hotels

A PROJECT I WOULD NOT WANT TO REPEAT!

Whilst a number of strategic leaders within the international hospitality industry can say that they have opened new hotels, I suspect that few have had the experience of closing a large, successful hotel for a period of two years, during which time it is completely renovated. Yet that is the challenge faced by John Stauss, Regional Vice President of Four Seasons Hotels and Resorts and General Manager of its London Hotel.

I first interviewed John in April 2006 for the research project, The Hospitality Leadership Excellence Survey, I was undertaking with Bournemouth University. He struck me then, as he again did when I spoke with him in connection with this book, as a quietly spoken, courteous gentleman. Indeed, his approach to leadership reminds me very much of one theme of the book, *Good to Great* by Jim Collins, which was given to me by another successful leader from the luxury hotel sector, Jasminder Singh from Radisson Edwardian Hotels (featured in Chapter 1.6). The book sought to identify how a good company can become a great one and, in doing so, found that such companies are invariably led by an executive who *'builds enduring greatness through a paradoxical blend of personal humility and professional will'*. John is not comfortable speaking about himself, yet his approach to leadership is one we can all learn a great deal from.

He started in the hospitality industry at an early age, as many of us did, including James Horler, from the previous chapter. In John's case, he remembers the exciting moment when, as a 15 year old, he was promoted from washing pots and pans to washing dishes! From such beginnings he worked his way to the front of house and then on to various management positions. During this period he attended a hotel school in Switzerland before moving on to work in the Caribbean. Interestingly, he has maintained an active interest in several Swiss hotel schools, including the Les Roches School of Hotel Management where he offers industry and academic advice to the students studying there. For example, in 2008 a group of students undertaking a project on organisational behaviour, asked him what advice he would give to students about to become leaders in the hospitality industry. He replied:

- Develop your unique management and leadership style, based on your own core values and the shifting expectations of the workplace.

- Continue to learn and develop at all times, both functional (technical) skills and generic leadership skills.

- Understand when to work as part of a team, and when to lead as an individual.

- Maintain a strong commitment, over the years, to think like both your guests and your staff.

- As economic cycles fluctuate, develop the necessary skills to lead both in the good times and the bad.

- Maintain absolute professionalism at all times.

- Always practise impeccable ethics, including social responsibility.

- Be adaptable, because the world in which we live and work is constantly changing and all successful leaders demonstrate an ongoing ability to be flexible, regardless of the circumstances.

Back to John's career in our industry: he joined Four Seasons nearly 30 years ago and has been General Manager of its London hotel for 15 years, as well as having a role overseeing a number of hotels across Europe, and beyond. In 2005 he was recognised as being the UK's Hotelier of the Year. In his book, *'Four Seasons, The Story of a Business Philosophy',* Isadore Sharp, the company's founder, remembers offering John his first general manager post in 1989 when he asked him if he would like to co-ordinate the building of a new Four Seasons resort on the small island of Nevis, two miles southeast of St Kitts in the Caribbean.

Although John had previously worked in Mustique and St Lucia, he had never even heard of Nevis. However, he consulted his wife and agreed to the appointment so long as he could have a goat (his wife was expecting their second child and wanted to ensure a plentiful supply of milk!). The resort opened in February 1991 and, under John's tenure, was voted the best hotel in the world by Conde Nast Traveller in 1995. It also proved the template for Four Seasons subsequently establishing hotels in the world's most exotic, but underdeveloped, areas.

John has faced many challenges over the years, but none more so than when, in September 2008, he was charged with closing his London hotel for a two-year renovation period. Planning for the closure actually commenced two years before the work started, when permission had to be secured from Westminster Council and the hotel sold from the, then, owner to another who would embrace the renovation. The Four Seasons business model is that they do not actually own any hotels; rather they manage them on management contracts of up to 50 years. Once planning permission was granted and the hotel sold, it was partially demolished, to be rebuilt to provide the highest levels of guest services and comfort.

In driving forward such a major project, I was interested in what leadership skills John found were particularly required. He explained that his most significant challenges were to clarify and communicate answers to the two big questions: *'what do we want to achieve?'* and, very importantly, *'why are we doing it?'*. After all, the hotel had been trading successfully for the previous 40 years, so why change! John condensed his leadership role, in relation to this major project, into explaining the vision to all the stakeholders and achieving their 'buy-in'. Once approval and finance had been secured, the two main groups he had to consider were the hotel's staff and its regular customers – many of whom were to be affected greatly by such a lengthy closure.

Four Seasons Hotels enjoys very high levels of guest loyalty. Isadore Sharp explains that, from opening the first hotel in Toronto in 1961, *"I approached the business of inn keeping from a customer's perspective. I was the host, and the customers were my houseguests. If we give them good value, they will unhesitatingly pay what they think it's worth. That was the first strategy, and it continues to this day."* Such an approach results in the likes of Larry King saying, *"I have a great deal of respect for Isadore Sharp and Four Seasons. I stay at their hotels all the time."* More details about Isadore Sharpe and his leadership are included in Chapter 1.6.

As far as the London hotel was concerned, many guests had returned annually for the past 25 years for, say, Wimbledon or the Chelsea Flower Show, whilst others used the hotel on a more routine, monthly, basis. Yet, whilst it was situated in a prime location, on Park Lane, the hotel's facilities did not match the physical product of other Four Seasons flagship hotels in, for example, New York, Paris or Hong Kong. Some guests had been saying for years that the hotel required renovation, yet when they got what they had been asking for, many were not too happy and posed the question *"Where am I going to stay for the next two years?"*.

Finding an acceptable solution for those guests was one of the major challenges for John and his staff, not least because before the hotel closed it had stored luggage and personal belongings for 82 regular guests and actual beds for 11! John, therefore, had to discuss the matter with each of these most loyal guests at the end of their last stay before the renovation commenced. Most agreed for John to find another London luxury hotel that could accommodate their specific needs, including storing their goods and chattels. To make matters more difficult, three of the 82 guests were adamant that they would not return to London until the hotel re-opened and so asked that their belongings be stored in the temporary office accommodation John and his small team of six were working from during the renovation!

It is a reflection of the close association Four Seasons has with their guests that some found their last stay at the London hotel to be very difficult. Seeing captains of industry becoming openly emotional as they checked out for the last time was stressful for everyone, including the hotel staff who experienced it. Even John was surprised at the reaction of some guests; how strongly some felt about the hotel experience. He explains this as being due to the fact that many guests relate hotels to milestones in their lives; perhaps their child's school-leaving dinner or the fact that the guest had concluded the business deal of their lifetime at the hotel. Nonetheless, the emotions some displayed were surprising for all concerned. Yet John believes that we all need new experiences to act as learning opportunities to keep us fresh in our roles – be it as a general manager or a hotel receptionist.

The process of saying, albeit temporary, farewell to loyal guests and of finding them alternative London accommodation begs the question whether they will return to the newly-renovated hotel two years later. Certainly, the three whose belongings are being stored over the period will have to! Yet John is not naïve enough to believe that some will not become well-settled in the other luxury hotels they are now using. The absence of these, he hopes, will be balanced to some extent by other Four Seasons regular international guests who, he knows, never used the London hotel because it was not considered up to the physical standard of others elsewhere in the world. In the meantime, he is heartened by the number of past guests who, when in London, ring him up and invite him to their new hotels for a coffee and to receive a progress report on how the renovation is progressing.

As well as the guest implications surrounding the closure, John's other major challenge was to find the best possible outcomes for the hotel's 350 staff. Four Seasons is a company that has been developed upon a foundation of trust and empowerment: very much Isadore Sharp's personal values. John believes that its recipe for success, and the reason for its longevity, is that the people who have been successful with the company are those that create, and operate within, a trust-based environment. There certainly appears to be justification for that claim as, not only has the company been recognised in the Caterer and Hotelkeeper's 'Best Places to Work in Hospitality' awards, but the Fortune Magazine in America has named Four Seasons as one of the top 100 companies to work for in America for the past 10 years.

A real-life example of the respect Four Seasons has for its staff was demonstrated following the terrorist attacks on 9/11. The London hotel that John manages relies heavily on guests from North America and, at that time, almost overnight, occupancy levels plummeted. Operating costs had to be reduced, most notably labour costs. However, rather than make an executive decision that would have impacted on the lives on his employees, many of whom were low income earners who relied entirely on their weekly pay cheque, John called an employee general meeting of his 350 staff of over 40 nationalities. He explained the situation the hotel was facing and offered them the choice of reducing the labour bill by the necessary 20 per cent by either making a fifth of the staff, the most recently recruited, redundant, or by all the staff going on a voluntary four-day week and taking the fifth day out of the holiday fund. A spontaneous show of hands indicated, without exception, all the staff chose to take the four-day week option, rather than have some their colleagues lose their jobs. Even staff who had worked in the hotel for over 20 years chose to protect those who had only worked there for a matter of weeks.

So, bearing in mind the culture that existed within the hotel, it is not surprising that John was at pains to put in place supportive procedures for his staff leading up to the lengthy closure. Again, just like the communications between the hotel and its owners, bankers and guests, he started sharing his vision with the staff before it was known if and when the hotel might close. It was crucial that they all understood the impact it was to have on their lives; they may not like what was to happen, or indeed recognise the need for it, but if they were kept fully in the picture they were much more likely to accept its inevitability and work with the hotel to ensure a smooth transition.

The support process for the staff was multi-layered: firstly, personal coaches were engaged to work with every member of the team. It was recognised that, although the service they provided within the hotel was of the highest standard, many of the staff did not appreciate the abilities they had. The coaches, therefore, helped them to recognise and list their skills and knowledge, whilst also training them in promoting their employability within an interview situation. Further specialists were then engaged to train the staff in composing CVs that would be attractive to potential future employers. The final aspect of the support process was to hold a job fair within the hotel, at which employers were invited to meet with the Four Seasons employees to discuss work opportunities with them. The fair saw over 50 companies, including those from other hotels, London clubs and the retail sector (including Harrods), assemble in the hotel's ballroom to present their opportunities.

John's goal was to ensure that 90 per cent of his staff who wanted another job found acceptable employment. In the event, more than that succeeded in doing so. One third transferred to other Four Seasons hotels and resorts across the world, with the remaining two-thirds preferring to remain in London for personal reasons. Some decided to take the opportunity to leave employment altogether; some to look after ageing parents; another to join an archaeological team on a survey overseas; some to study. John had estimated that 25 per cent of the staff would leave before the hotel closed but, in the event, nobody did. Although the majority had another job to go on to, they all said that they wanted to work in the hotel right up to the final day.

Throughout the process, collective consultation was undertaken in respect of the redundancy arrangements. It is a legal requirement when a company is making more than 20 employees redundant that, in addition to them having several one-to-one interviews with HR, elected departmental representatives also present their case in group discussions with senior management - collective consultation. In Four Seasons' case, this involved a staff member, not always the most senior person, representing each of the 20 departments of the hotel. It was a huge responsibility for those chosen by their colleagues to undertake this role – with each member of staff wanting the best redundancy package secured for them. However, all parties took the process seriously and constructively and, although some requests could not be approved due to UK employment law, compromise solutions were found in all cases, often by rewarding all staff, rather than merely specific groups or individuals.

With the hotel closed and the renovation work now well underway, John looks back at the build-up to the closure and describes it as *"an exciting project, but one I would not want to repeat!"*. He sees it as having been a unique learning opportunity to understand what employees' needs and priorities are, how their job fits into their lives, and how they often have to balance their family circumstances with the necessity of earning a secure income. As the three year process evolves, the early emotional highs and lows have abated and he is now able to adopt a more practical, pragmatic approach. Yet all aspects of the project have combined to offer John a powerful life lesson to add to the others he has benefited from his career in the hotel industry.

2.3 STUART BOWERY

Cluster General Manager, Marriott Hotels

MONEY MATTERS

After 29 years continuous service with Marriott Hotels and Resorts, in its current or previous guises, Stuart Bowery is certainly the right man to take the brand forward during difficult financial times. Like Four Seasons Hotels, featured elsewhere in this book, Marriott do not own hotels; rather they manage them on, say, 25 year agreements on behalf of their owners. In Stuart's case, not only is he the General Manager of County Hall – a luxury, 200 bedroom, five-star hotel sited on the Thames, opposite Big Ben – he also has the role of Cluster General Manager (GM) for seven other Marriott hotels in London.

Having met with Stuart and discussed his job with him, I think it is fair to say that, in addition to managing County Hall, he faces two other major leadership roles: providing support and guidance to the GMs from his seven cluster operations; and liaising with the hotels' owners – a consortium of financiers.

Providing leadership for his fellow GMs, all of whom have different levels of experience and personal strengths, requires Stuart to adopt differing approaches. For those more experienced, he will give them more latitude to develop their own hotel's positioning and identity so long as they do so within Marriott's established processes. The GMs with less industry experience may need more support, not least before and during visits from their hotel's owners, who are required to demonstrate to their own funders, the bankers, that they are conducting regular reviews of their business.

The operating model for some hotels has certainly changed since I entered the hospitality industry over 35 years ago. Then, hotels were usually managed by traditional owner-operators who took a long-term view in terms of business development. Here, in Marriott's case, hotels are owned by property investment institutions and consortiums, with asset managers leveraging their property portfolio to maximise profit potential.

I was interested what effect this *modus operandi* had on the hotels' GMs. Were they faced with pressures to cut costs, at the expense of service levels, in order to increase profits? Take Stuart's own hotel, County Hall, as an example, how has he faced up to the inevitable reduced occupancy resulting from the recession? In fact, he explained, occupancy levels for all his eight hotels, have held up pretty well – achieving an average of around 80-85 per cent, with periods of up to 97 per cent for some of the Central London properties.

County Hall, as an iconic building, benefits from a strong cultural history. In fact, all its staff, even the 30 per cent agency staff, are encouraged to adopt a sense of pride in both their jobs and the building they work in, with cultural training offered to inform all permanent staff of the history of their place of work and its surroundings. As Stuart suggested, *"All the world is a stage and all our staff are actors on that stage when they engage with their customers"*. He is well aware that guest satisfaction and, hence, retention can be greatly enhanced by customer-facing staff who are willing and able to advise a guest on how they can best enjoy their stay in a hotel with such an interesting history.

As for Stuart himself, his contribution to the success of his hotel, and those within his cluster, is founded upon his deep understanding of the industry, and a keen commercial awareness of industry norms. With this knowledge he is well-placed to present strategic plans to the hotel owners, based upon current and forecast market share performance. Indeed, presenting credible commercial reports to the asset managers in respect of all eight of Stuart's hotels is a most significant aspect of his job: explaining what, for example, will be the impact next year, and beyond, of the costs that have inevitably had to be taken out during the recession.

Take the budget for 2009, drawn up in the autumn of the previous year when the extent of the recession had not been fully realised. Whilst the budgeted sales against the previous year had been reduced (by 3 per cent in the first quarter; 2 per cent in the second quarter; flat in the third quarter; with some growth forecast for the remainder of the year), by the beginning of the year it was obvious that this estimate was wildly optimistic – things were going to be much worse than expected! In a meeting with the owners, Stuart called upon his past experience of the industry, and the credibility that afforded him, to achieve an agreement to accept a much more realistic forecast turnover. In the event, his hotels have exceeded budget to the delight of the owners – it is always better to under-promise and over-deliver!

It is in such potentially challenging meetings that Stuart can best support his other GMs – taking a leadership position as the principle communication between them and their hotel owners. By way of an example, he told me of a recent meeting he attended in which a young financier was demanding that one of Stuart's GMs review the operation of one, underperforming, aspect of his hotel. Stuart was able to defend his GM by explaining that guests who are paying £300 per night have an expectation of appropriate levels of facilities and service. The restaurant may not be hugely profitable some evenings but that is not sufficient justification to close it. In such instances, Stuart seeks to adopt a conciliatory approach in order to defuse any potential conflict between hotel owner and hotel operator.

And of course, Stuart's own hotel must be seen to perform, just like the other seven in his cluster, which adds to the leadership challenges associated with his multi-faceted role. Not only do the owners have full access to every aspect of the business, but the other GMs see not only the financial performance of County Hall, but also the results of all the quality assurance scoring undertaken by Marriott. Hence, when I asked Stuart what attributes are essential for a leader within the hospitality industry, top of his list was to act as a role model. Not only should leaders consider how others see them on a day-to-day operational level, but also from a longer-term strategic perspective.

For a GM it is crucial, he believes, that effective, positive communications are maintained with the hotel's executive committee in order to keep senior managers focused on seeking and achieving targets designed to drive the business forward. For Stuart, of course, that responsibility extends to the seven other GMs he has responsibility for.

Indeed, one of his major personal motivational factors is being able to influence the performance of the entire cluster of hotels – which he appears to do with great success.

2.4 GRAHAM OLDS

Operations Director,
Holroyd Howe Independent

GOING STRATEGIC

Graham Olds' initial career aspirations, at the age of 17, were hardly of stellar proportions: he decided that he wanted to be an assistant chef in a job without any responsibilities. He achieved that modest objective and then decided that he wanted to get into hospitality management – but only as an assistant manager!

He has continued this strategy – taking one step forward and becoming comfortable with his new role before looking for another challenge – throughout his career. He progressed from managerial jobs in outside events to those in industrial catering, before entering the contract catering sector. Again, he made steady progression from small operations to larger ones and then to an operations manager running 12 contracts before eventually being responsible for 35 units as a general manager.

Prior to joining Holroyd Howe in 2004, Graham's career progression had been in a traditional vertical direction but his new employers offered him the opportunity to take a sideways step into sales. They were looking for someone with extensive operational experience, who had the potential to convert that background into a successful sales role. It was accepted by both parties that his total lack of sales experience was a risk but the company believed that Graham had the personality and positive attitude to make the transition – given sufficient time and support.

From a leadership perspective, it was very interesting to hear from Graham how Holroyd Howe went about converting him from an operator to a sales manager. As suggested by the name, the company was formed in 1997 by Nick Howe and Rick Holroyd. Graham describes them fondly as being exceptional leaders, albeit both with very different approaches. Rick is the strategist, whilst Nick's strengths lie more in terms of human interaction. For Graham, especially during his transition into a sales role, it was their understanding of his personal needs that was the catalyst for his success. He was encouraged to grow gradually into his new role. During the first year he was never pressurised, rather their approach was *Take as long as it takes and don't be disappointed if you make mistakes along the way.* Graham believes that they understood how he develops best: by learning and then taking the learning further – just as he had built his career to date from humble beginnings as an assistant chef (with no responsibility!).

How often do we see in our industry, as in others, people being expected to step up to the plate without the necessary support and sufficient time to make that transition? As far as Nick Howe and Rick Holroyd were concerned, they had confidence in Graham and were prepared to wait for the results to materialise. And, in time, they certainly did: near the end of Graham's first year in sales he landed two contracts on two consecutive days, which were duly celebrated in champagne. Their belief was that, for a sales person to be able to sell, he or she must understand both the client needs and the operational implications of what they are selling. Graham's mandate was to create a bespoke service offer for each potential client and then to go out and make the sale. Their patient strategy certainly harvested fruit, with Graham securing 13 new contracts in the following 18 months.

So, after a steady advancement through unit manager to operations manager to sales manager, Graham was happily bringing in business to Holroyd Howe when, in December 2007, the company merged with BaxterStorey; making the new, combined business the largest independent contract caterer in the UK. Rick Holroyd became Managing Director within BaxterStorey and Nick Howe started a new subsidiary company, Holroyd Howe Independent, providing food services solely to independent schools, in which he offered Graham the post of Operations Director. Moving from an operational to a strategic leadership role was a big step and Graham was well aware that he must not allow his natural reactive enthusiasm to overly influence his decision. Strategic leadership calls for a different skill-set; not least, as Graham realised, that in this new role he would have to complement Nick's skills with a more strategic approach. As a director, Graham would have to balance his natural, 'can-do' attitude, formed from a lifetime in the catering industry, with the responsibilities of a company director. Understanding the challenge of moving from operational to strategic leadership, and learning how Graham took that step, offers a valuable learning opportunity for others who aspire to achieve senior positions in our industry.

So what are the differences between operational and strategic leadership, I asked him. He explained that he must now make time to stand back and take a longer-term perspective of the business. An operation like Holroyd Howe Independent has not only a service to provide three times a day, but also must be in a fit shape to deliver that same service in six months, or five years, time. The danger for directors is that they get too involved in the day-to-day operations. This, he feels, is particularly dangerous in the independent school sector, where catering is seen as an integral part of school life and, hence, clients become very interested in the fine detail of the service and how it impacts on the smooth running of their school. The caterers are recognised as contributing to the school in a number of ways: socially, with a pastoral care role; financially, in terms of the impact on the school budget; and academically, in the realisation that 'well-fed children learn better'. The director must take all these factors into consideration when mapping out a medium-to-long-term strategy for the company; not least to ensure that on-site catering managers build supportive relationships with the schools, whilst retaining allegiance to their employer – the contractor.

Another higher-level responsibility Graham now has is to ensure that his operations team is encouraged to contribute to the strategic direction of the company. He recognises that he was successful in Holroyd Howe because he was not tied down; rather, he was given space to develop and be creative. Now as a director of Holroyd Howe Independent, he must ensure that his operational managers are afforded the same opportunities. Are there the right people in the right positions to take the business forward? Do those people have the time and inclination to identify and realise opportunities within their regions, or are they too constrained and process-driven from the centre? Are Nick and Graham encouraging creative, visionary thinking across the company and empowering their managers to take decisions, even calculated risks, which will ensure continuing success for the company?

Graham is certainly aware that it would be all too easy for someone with ultimate responsibility for the long-term viability of a company to concentrate too much on processes, hence stifling the energy and enthusiasm within its engine room. Strategic leaders must use their ultimate authority to encourage an open and challenging culture within their organisations – acknowledging the value of individual initiative and rewarding those that use it for the development of the business.

Now almost two years into post as director of Holroyd Howe Independent, I asked Graham how he has adapted to his new role. He told me that it had not been easy to curb his natural enthusiasm in order to take a more strategic, long-term view. He has forced himself to stand back and become divorced from his operational inclinations and to think very carefully about the implications of all his decisions on the future of the company. Having done that, he can then apply his inherent passion into enthusing those that have to deliver the service to the end-users. A balance must be struck between the need for visionary planning and the delivery of an exceptional daily service by highly motivated, customer-driven staff.

Not surprisingly for a person who likes to move forward step-by-step, Graham characterises the approach a strategic leader must take:

- Distinguish between short, medium and long-term goals and then allocate them into separate pigeonholes.

- Make time to concentrate on each pigeonhole in a structured way.

- Organise your mind to move seamlessly from one objective to another, never leaving any one of them unfinished.

- Consider the implications of each goal in terms of product, service, people and finances.

- Devise implementation strategies to achieve each goal that will contribute to the success of the company, moving forward.

I think Graham would concede that *going strategic* has been the steepest learning curve of his career, but one that has brought him the greatest rewards.

2.5 GARY DODDS

Regional Vice President of Human Resources, Marriott Hotels

A FAMILY CULTURE

'Family' means a great deal to Gary Dodds: not only his own, highlighted by the photographs on the wall alongside the meeting table in his office, but also an employment culture, based on family values, that recognises each member of staff for the unique contribution they can make to the success of the group. Indeed, when Gary recalls his journey from a youthful individual who, in his early HR career was interested in civil and welfare rights, to his current role as Regional Vice President of Human Resources for Marriott's 82 business operations in the UK, Ireland, Middle East and Africa, it becomes apparent that he has mainly worked for companies with a strong family history and governance.

Most of Gary's years in the hospitality industry have been spent with two large corporations – InterContinental Hotels, previously owned by the Tsutsumi family of Japan, and The Peninsula Hotel Group (and its parent company, The Hong Kong & Shanghai Hotels), which was started in the early 1880s by the Kadoosie family and is still run by their descendents today. Peninsula's emphasis on the family is evident by the home page of its current website that features a screen size photograph of a group of company employees holding young children, all dressed as chefs. His career has also included working as Director of Human Resources for a hotel in Bahrain owned by the Crown Prince of the country for ITT Sheraton; and developing his own family's country house hotel in Devon. It was seven years ago, when Gary was working for a family-run HR consultancy firm in America, that he was contacted by Mr Tsutsumi who put him in touch with the Deputy Chairman of Marriott, Bill Teifel, which subsequently led to his current job with them. For Gary, it was like coming home: he felt that his entire previous career had prepared him for what he found in Marriott. He describes feeling in some of his early jobs like a salmon swimming upstream to spawn – battling against the current in a business that recognised the importance of people but did not always 'walk the talk'. Yet, in Marriott he was experiencing the thrill of swimming down the rapids in a culture that represented his own beliefs and values so closely.

As expanded in Chapter 1.6, in 1963 when Bill Marriott Jnr assumed control of the company, he asked his father, who founded the business in 1927, what he should concentrate on in order to continue its success: percentage occupancy; room revenue; or rack rates? The reply was simple: *"Treat everyone with dignity and respect. Do not hire people because of their colour, race or religion – hire the right person for the job and then treat them as family. Do not lead your people; lead through your people"*. It was Bill Marriott Snr's firm belief that people respond positively to being treated as an individual which, in turn, transfers to the way they treat the customer – who feel they will be truly welcomed back. Hence, the Marriott secret of success was to concentrate on repeat business because that drives revenue, return on investment for owners, and ultimately profitability. Genuinely treating staff with care, dignity and respect as the driver of business success was the company's philosophy then and, Gary explained, continues as a cornerstone of its culture to this day.

More recently, in 2003, Stephen Marriott, Senior Vice President of Company Culture made a presentation to 900 general managers in which he demonstrated that, over the previous five years, in hotels where this culture was practised one hundred per cent by a general manager, it cascaded down to all leadership levels and, as a consequence, staff opinion scores rose and remained high; which was reflected in guest satisfaction levels rising; which ultimately resulted in increased company profitability and return on investment for owners. Conversely, where associates do not feel valued, it has the opposite effect – right down to the bottom line. In statistical terms, labour turnover in Marriott's UK hotels is typically 26 per cent across the region, compared with many in the sector with averages of 40 per cent; turnover of managers is only 17 per cent; and, world-wide, the average general manager has been with the company for 17 years. The fundamental point Gary makes is that Bill Marriott Snr's vision still permeates throughout the company's 3,000 hotels, employing 169,000 staff members in 69 countries; and has proved to be an enduring influence on the culture of the company to this date.

Indeed, it was the founding family that created the nine core leadership competences that are still used to assess managerial candidates during recruitment; that form the basis of the company's management development programmes; and are the principles against which continuing performance is evaluated. These are:

1. Organisational learner
2. Technical expertise
3. Developing others
4. Fostering teamwork and relationships
5. Focussing on customers
6. Communicating openly
7. Managing work execution
8. Managing change
9. Leading

Personally, I am sure that many other organisations, in our industry and elsewhere, have a largely similar set of competences. They are certainly admirable 'management speak'. Yet 'actions speak louder than words' and employees will certainly not buy into a culture based upon such fine-sounding principles unless the organisation practices what it preaches, at all levels of management. So, does Marriott actually demonstrate the value it places on every member of staff (or 'associate' as it terms them as a means of reinforcing the concept of shared responsibility and, hence, mutual dependency)? Here are some of the initiatives that Gary told me about:

• Every hotel has an Associate Relations Committee on which representatives, nominated by their peers, meet on a regular basis. The committee elects its own chair and secretary, and the hotel's General Manager and HR Director are required to attend every meeting to brief the representatives on any business information that affects the hotel and its staff and to listen to, and address, any collective concerns and issues.

- Additionally, the General Manager must regularly hold a 'Town Hall Meeting', to which all staff are invited to attend. Moreover, when a Regional HR Manager visits the hotel he or she will often hold a similar meeting, but without the presence of any members of the management team. Staff at either meeting who raise queries are guaranteed a response within 24 hours.

- On a global scale, a scheme exists called the Guarantee of Fair Treatment whereby any employee can contact the GFT Centre in the USA, openly or anonymously, to report that they feel they have been treated unreasonably by their supervisor or manager. Every complaint is passed to the HR leader of the employee's region who is required to instigate an investigation. Every complaint is responded to, even if it was submitted anonymously by upsetofdubai@hotmail.com! I asked Gary if this opportunity is often abused and he estimated that for every malicious complaint there are nine genuine submissions – although the vast majority of those are eventually proved to have been caused as a result of poor communications or misunderstanding. Nonetheless, the associate's voice has been heard and registered and if anything has truly been handled poorly it will be resolved and the associate advised what action has been taken; the objective being to ensure associate satisfaction.

Another Marriott scheme that Gary was very proud of was *Spirit to Serve*, which gives every employee the opportunity to support local communities or charities. Indeed, every hotel worldwide typically supports at least two local charities every year and gives its staff the chance to become involved in associated activities. Whilst not seeking media coverage for these events, the company is well aware that building relationships within the community can realise business benefits: both in terms of enhanced staff engagement and increased loyalty from local organisations. Many of Marriott's employees world-wide do embrace the *Spirit to Serve* and 12 of the most inspiring stories are featured in an annual booklet produced by the company; as well as those involved being flown, with their families, to America to receive a global award in a ceremony attended by the entire Marriott family.

The company expects every leader to act as a Guardian of the Marriott culture and so, every two years, Gary gathers HR directors together for a three-day programme of shared learning and personal development. One half-day is devoted to a *Spirit to Serve* event, such as visiting a local hospice, chatting to its residents, and serving an afternoon tea to them. Gary tells a particularly moving story, demonstrating the power of service, which happened when he took a group of 40 HR directors from the Middle East and Africa region to a home for abandoned or severely handicapped elderly people in Alexandria, Egypt. Gary felt it would offer an appropriate venue for his multi-faith group of HR leaders to meet and serve lunch to its 60 residents, all of whom were over 70 years of age. It was certainly a powerful experience for those who attended, not least for one of them – a 35 year old, strong, tough Saudi man, who was seen with tears streaming down his face whilst he fed a 90 year old lady who had no arms.

You see, for Gary that one story encapsulated all the lessons and beliefs he has amassed throughout his lifetime's employment as a leader in the hospitality industry: the unique importance of every individual; the need to treat everyone with dignity and respect; the power of the family unit; the rich diversities of different cultures; and the benefits to be realised by serving others, both within a business and within a community.

2.6 STEPHEN PHILLIPS

Operations Manager,
Brookwood Partnership

FINDING HIS SPIRITUAL HOME

It is apparent that Stephen Phillips has found his spiritual home in the Brookwood Partnership. After over 30 years employment in the contract catering sector he now works in a company that exemplifies many of his own values, both in terms of food production and inter-personal relationships.

Stephen studied for a Higher National Diploma in Hotel and Catering Management at Hollings College in Manchester at the same time as I was taking the same qualification at Blackpool College. In those days there were only two educational establishments that offered a degree in hotel and catering (the term 'hospitality management' had not been coined in the early 1970s) and they were the Universities of Surrey and Strathclyde. Hence, most of us who aspired to take up a managerial post in the industry were directed towards an HND.

Following the three years training, many hoped to be invited to take up a junior management post with a large hotel group, perhaps Trust Houses Forte or British Transport Hotels. But not Stephen: he was obviously a 'foodie' at heart, even in his formative years in the industry. Rather than seeking to put into practice the management theory he learnt at college, he elected to develop his craft skills before taking his first step on the management ladder. Hence, he joined the BBC as a cook, working for two years at Broadcasting House before joining their own management development programme.

That was the start of a successful career in contract catering that culminated in him working for a large company as a regional director. The remuneration package was good, the company car was a BMW but, after 20 years with the company, the true caterer in him began to ask some searching questions. Was he really working in the food industry? Had he become too far removed from his true vocation? He certainly spent a lot of his time considering matters financial and was heavily involved in union negotiations, but he was coming to realise that he wasn't talking about food from one week to the next, nor was he interfacing with those that bought and consumed the food.

However, at about that time fate took a hand as his company began a down-sizing process that involved making all the regional directors redundant. Stephen thought long and hard about seeking employment outside the contract catering sector until he saw a full page advert for operational managers in the Caterer and Hotelkeeper magazine. The company was the Brookwood Partnership – a relatively new provider, largely in the independent school sector, that described itself as *'a caring company'*. Stephen recalls being impressed by the claim, if also a little sceptical. However, that scepticism soon disappeared when he first met Kate Martin, one of the company founders, and realised *"These people really mean it. They are not just saying the right things!"*. That was three years ago and he has obviously not changed his opinion since then. To Stephen, Brookwood is a company that practises the values he holds dear. It reminds him why he entered the hospitality industry in the first place.

He is, though, the first to admit that Brookwood is not the cheapest contract caterer offering its services in the education sector. For example, each operations manager oversees only ten contracts. This is an expensive ratio but it means that they can provide close support for both their kitchen teams and their clients. Stephen takes great pride in the fact that he knows the first name of the majority of the kitchen assistants working in the kitchens he is responsible for. When he visits a unit he makes a point of chatting to each of them before he sees the catering manager – getting to know a bit about them and their families; making them feel valued as part of the Brookwood family.

This close association with company staff is an expectation of Brookwood area managers that is particularly well demonstrated by the induction process they embark on upon joining the company. Indeed, Stephen is particularly aware of the positive impact a structured induction can have on a new employee; as well as recalling the opposite effect he experienced personally in his early managerial career. He well remembers joining a small company, as an area manager, that had around 40 contracts in the Twickenham area of London. His arrival interview consisted on his new boss saying *"There is a list of your sites. Here are the keys for your Cortina. Come back in a week and let us know how you got on"*.

It is true to say that one learns as many leadership lessons from bad example as from good, and for Stephen it had to be a fast learning curve with that company. For example, none of the three area managers were given access to the financial information relating to their contract sites. He recalls interviews where the client wanted to discuss aspects of the catering account – which Stephen could only comment on by reading the figures from his side of the client's desk. One of the skills he did learn in that job was to read figures upside-down – an ability that he had to put into practice on more than once occasion since!

Having learnt from experience how <u>not</u> to induct someone into a job, he now takes particular care to adopt better practice with his staff. He told me, as an example, that a new operations manager had recently joined his team, for whom he spent a great deal of time preparing a thorough induction programme. Initially, he wanted her to spend two weeks becoming fully acquainted with her sites and, in particular, to appreciate the importance Brookwood gives to the food on the plate – ultimately what they are judged upon. The next stage involved briefings on aspects of her role, such as HR and finance.

After that, she worked in a site undertaking every job required of each member of the kitchen team. Doing so, Stephen believes, allows her to experience first-hand how her people actually feel doing their work in a kitchen. Indeed, she subsequently asked to extend this experience by spending one day working in every kitchen on her patch. One wonders how many other hospitality leaders spend as much time and effort preparing new staff for their roles.

Stephen feels that actually working alongside kitchen teams helps to build close relationships with them and goes a long way to dispelling the potential mental image of area managers merely 'driving around in cars and drinking cups of coffee'. Indeed, he hopes to extend the practice by encouraging members of the Brookwood central administration team to spend a day or two working in a kitchen. Doing so, he believes, will promote a better understanding in support staff of what school catering involves: the pressure of producing food for children from a hot kitchen, over a short, intense meal period. Not only will the administrative and kitchen team members have a mental picture of each other when they subsequently speak on the phone, but they will better understand the importance of each member of the Brookwood team.

Stephen firmly believes that catering is a people-oriented business and, to be successful, you have to be a people-person. You may be the best cook in the world, he argues, but if you cannot get on with, and influence, people you haven't got a chance. To Stephen, one of his principle leadership roles is to facilitate opportunities for that to happen in Brookwood.

Another role is to enhance levels of communication across the company. He believes it is vital for any company to be transparent with its staff and to seek every opportunity to encourage effective communication, in every direction. Brookwood produces a regular staff magazine, *The Brookwood Bite,* and Stephen is at pains to ensure that it reaches every member of the kitchen teams. A further recent initiative is Brookwood Breaks – weekly site meetings that operation managers hold with their kitchen teams. Yet even with such open communication channels, Stephen admits that there are still members of staff who complain about not being told enough, or not having their voice heard.

This led me to ask him how he can make, say, a general assistant working only a couple of hours a day proud to work for Brookwood. By means of an explanation, he told me about a contract they had recently taken over from one of the large contract caterers. The first time Stephen visited the school, the Head Teacher asked to see him and gave him a long list of things he was unhappy about. The unit catering manager left, stating that the staff were useless, "a bad bunch". Certainly the morale within the kitchen was low, with the staff having little pride in the food they were providing for the children.

Stephen gave the contract a good deal of his personal attention, with the staff saying they had seen more of him in the first two weeks than they had seen the previous company's operations manager in two years! A new catering manager was engaged and a menu based upon fresh ingredients was introduced. The servery presentation was improved and the staff got new uniforms and individual training programmes. Soon, heads began to rise as the complaints they were used to getting turned into compliments. Although they were working harder, using less convenience food, they had a pride in the product they were producing. As Stephen describes, they were now recognised as professional caterers providing food their customers appreciated, and not just the 'units of production' they had been with their previous employer. That is what motivates people, he asserts – even a general assistant working only a couple of hours a day.

Still on the theme of personal motivation, I asked Stephen what motivated him, especially within his role in Brookwood. Perhaps not surprisingly, he listed similar factors to the general assistants he had just been describing: being respected; feeling valued; being listened to; and believing in the values of the company. He feels strongly that there is a social value in feeding children healthy, nutritious food and he believes that Brookwood take that social responsibility seriously.

Indeed, their *'Planet Matters'* initiative involves many aspects of Corporate Social Responsibility, such as having policies on recycling waste and animal welfare. They only use free-range eggs, dolphin-friendly tuna, and other fish products that are listed as not being over-fished. Whilst this matters personally to Stephen, he also recognises it as a positive unique selling point for the business. As Anita Roddick, the founder of Body Shop once said, *"Being good is good business"*.

Being seen as having a social conscience can also go some way to countering the negative image of the catering industry. Stephen believes that hospitality is increasingly being recognised as a skilled profession but, in some people's mind, caterers are still considered to be servile, even subservient. He tells the story of a titled lady, a governor of an independent school at which Brookwood had the catering contract, asking them to provide a private dinner party for her. The guests, in their finery, were enjoying pre-dinner drinks on the patio and the chefs were preparing the food in the adjoining kitchen when, all of a sudden, the kitchen was plunged into darkness. The chef dashed out to enquire whether a fuse had blown, only to be told by the lady hostess, dismissively, *"No, I turned out the lights because my guests could see you all working in the kitchen"*.

Stephen surmises that the general public does not always appreciate what caterers can do in schools! The old-fashioned image of boiled cabbage and lumpy custard can still influence some people's perception of school dinners. Yet their customers, parents and children, these days are well-travelled and have more sophisticated tastes than ever before. Stephen had recently visited a school and noticed goats cheese and chorizo omelettes on the menu. He doubted whether such an unusual dish, with particularly strong flavours, would sell well – yet they flew off the servery!

A hospitality leader has a responsibility to counter the negative image of our industry that can have a serious effect on staff recruitment and, in cases where bad practice is adopted, staff retention. Our Sector Skills Council, People 1st, has identified that 'labour turnover across the sector is the highest of all sectors of the economy', yet far-sighted companies like the Brookwood Partnership are working hard to change the perception of the hospitality industry as being a poor employer. For Stephen, that involves not accepting sub-standard work; questioning inappropriate behaviour; adopting a caring and supportive attitude to staff; and providing opportunities for all staff to progress within their workplaces, should they aspire to do so. It is the leader's ultimate role to provide an example of behaviour for others to follow.

Certainly, from my meeting with Stephen, and my past knowledge of the Brookwood Partnership, there are examples of good practice within this company that our industry, and its image, can only benefit from.

2.7 DAVID HUGHES

General Manager, Premier Inn

LEADERSHIP DREAMS

As is often the case, David Hughes' first leadership lessons in the hotel industry were how <u>not</u> to treat people, as opposed to how to motivate and inspire them. Luckily, he chose the latter approach and became an exceptional leader – one of the most inspirational I interviewed for this book.

He started his career working in the reservations department of the Adelphi Hotel in his native Liverpool. It was during the time that the hotel featured in the 1997 BBC television series which branded it as the 'real-life Fawlty Towers'. David characterises his time there as 'learning how not to run a hotel'. It was, however, the circumstances surrounding his departure that had the most profound effect on him. He had only worked in the hotel for around six months when he was invited to take up another post in a rival hotel. It offered more responsibility and cash so, as a young man with a young family, he gave his week's notice to the Adelphi. The General Manager accepted his resignation and said that he could take up his new post immediately, without working his notice period – she would send the pay he was owed on to him. However, she never did, despite reminders from him.

For David, this experience made him think, for the first time, about how people holding leadership positions can influence, positively or negatively, the morale and motivation of their people. His subsequent career in our industry has been founded upon the belief that the leader is only as good as the people working in the business: if the people do not share the leader's dreams neither party will succeed. Unlike the Adelphi's GM, David appreciates the value of every member of his staff and understands how crucial it is for the leader to demonstrate that belief in every aspect of working life.

Thankfully, David experienced better leadership role models in the hotels in which he worked after leaving the Adelphi. From Chris Brown at the Moat House he learnt how important it is to address and overcome obstacles to the business without delay. Simon Matthews-Williams, owner and GM of the newly opened Crowne Plaza, demonstrated a deep pride in his hotel, even being seen by David picking up cigarette ends in the car park. Another mentor, Gary Laird, encouraged David to broaden his horizons and seek an appointment that offered more opportunities to develop his career. This advice led David to apply to join Travel Inn, a company with a culture that appealed to him; one he describes to me as *"We work hard but have fun and do not take ourselves as pretentiously as some of the large chains"*.

His first role with Travel Inn was to manage their new operation in Leeds – which he enjoyed enormously. However, after two and a half successful years he was finding commuting between his job and his family in Liverpool increasingly difficult and he was given the opportunity to move to his current hotel that sits proud alongside Albert Dock in his home city. At that time, it was an old Premier Lodge site, before the company merged with Travel Inn, and was seen as the poor relation of the central city hotel that had just won Hotel of the Year.

Arriving in December 2005, he inherited a team that he describes as 'being on their knees', believing themselves continuingly compared unfavourably to those working in the city centre hotel. Morale was low, fuelled by the lack of support between both hotel teams. Yet the hotel's location was stunning and David believed it had the potential to become the best hotel in Liverpool, perhaps the best in the whole of the parent company, Whitbread – his job, he realised, was to get his team to share that dream!

David talks a lot about dreams – that is not to say he is a dreamer, far from it, but he is a visionary. Moreover, critically, he has the ability to inspire his staff to join him on his journey. In his early days at Albert Dock the dream he shared was 'to be recognised as the best Premier Travel Inn in the UK' and within a mere six months they had begun to make their mark. By May 2006 their quality audit results were so impressive that the hotel received their first Whitbread Award – for continuous improvement.

The journey had begun but other milestones were ahead: to be recognised as a training centre for Premier Inn; to achieve the best brand audit scores; to smash sales and profit targets – all of which were conceived and set by his invigorated management team.

David explains that progress commences with the conception of ideas but then becomes the creation of shared values. In the case of his team at Albert Dock, none of the 60 or more staff members will now accept second-best. They understand that they can achieve their goals if they all combine together to deliver exceptional guest service. With the contribution of every team member, working within every department of the hotel, they believe they can gain the ultimate accolade – to be recognised as the very best operation in the whole of Whitbread. Each job contributes: for example, a dirty breakfast plate from the pot wash may form the last, and lasting, impression a departing guest has of the hotel. Behind every door, behind the scenes, is a sign encouraging staff members to *Do your job with dignity and pride.*

A fundamental tenet underpinning David's philosophy is that, as he says, all successful teams are built from within. Hence, he delights in encouraging internal career development and proudly told me that during the previous two years the hotel had seen 20 internal progressions. A particular example of such was Alison, who started work in the hotel as a junior member of the reception team. Her potential was immediately recognised by David who, within six months, had promoted her to be a team leader and 12 months after that invited her to open and run the hotel's new conference centre. Since then she has become Reception Manager and still has, David believes, the potential to progress even further within the company.

But the continuing progress of the Premier Inn at Albert Dock is not founded merely upon individual success. It is the team that is now driving forward improvements. When things go wrong, as we all know they sometimes do in our industry, the hotel rises as a whole to meet the challenge full-on. David describes it as a 'self-generating machine' and proudly explained to me an example of what he means by that phrase.

It was in December 2007, at a time when the hotel was being extended and some of the floors were closed for refurbishment. The hotel was full, including a conference for Whitbread managers from across the company, when, at 4.00 pm on a Friday, the entire third floor lost its TV signal. David was away, so the shift complement of 18 took the executive decision to open up the fourth floor, one that was being refurbished, and move all the third floor guests up one level. It was simply not acceptable, in the staff's mind, for their guests not to be able to use the televisions in their rooms. Within two hours all the fourth floor rooms had been cleaned, beds made and guests moved – all due to the initiative taken by the hotel staff. That was the point when David realised that his initial dream had been realised. Every member of staff now took ownership for his or her part in driving forward the business by providing an exceptional guest experience.

The week previous to my meeting with David, the hotel had won the Whitbread Business of the Year Award, so David's original dream has been realised. Yet he recognises that leadership is a journey, not a destination, so new dreams must now be set. Where is there to go, he asked me, after being recognised as the best business in a huge company like Whitbread? I suggested that his approach must now change from setting big targets, to concentrating on achieving smaller incremental improvements to the high standards they now deliver – Continuous Quality Improvement in management-speak.

I shared with him a leadership tip I learnt from Alastair Storey, Chairman of the UK's largest independent contract catering company, BaxterStorey. When Alastair visits his outlets and sees something that he feels could be improved he asks a member of staff *"Do you think that is the best we can do?"* What a cleverly crafted question. It makes the suggestion in an unthreatening, indirect, yet inclusive, way. The point is made and the staff member's opinion is sought. Who is going to answer *"Yes, that is the best we can do"*? The question almost demands the creation and ownership of a shared solution.

David fully appreciated the power and simplicity of the question and its potential to create the incremental improvements to the hotel he will be seeking in the future. The interview was closed with him announcing that the next year's mantra for the hotel will be 'Is that the best we can do?' It will certainly be interesting to see how much better David's team can actually get in the future.

2.8 PHIL SCOTT

General Manager, Premier Inn

CHANGING HEARTS AND MINDS

When Phil Scott took over the new Premier Inn in Manchester, just across the road from the Old Trafford football ground, he imagined that it would take six months to get the hotel running the way he wanted it. After all, he had a good deal of experience within the company, having worked in their hotels in London, Gatwick and, most recently, Liverpool. Little did he appreciate the task facing him and the 18 months of challenging work ahead.

The hotel had a history. Premier Inn had purchased it from the previous owners, Golden Tulip, in October 2007 and completed its brand conversion two months later. Prior to that, having formally been a Quality Hotel, the team had spent two years working on converting it from a three-star operation to achieve four-star status. In December, the 100 or so staff, many having worked at the hotel for many years, were called together to be told that it was now to be operated as a budget hotel, with the much-respected General Manager moving on and a new GM, Phil Scott, taking over the reins.

It is not difficult to imagine how the staff took the news. In their minds, all their hard work in developing the hotel's facilities and services to four-star standards had come to nought and they were now expected by the new owners, personified by the new GM, to deliver budget standards of service and product. Moreover, there was no further need for many of the team who fulfilled traditional roles incumbent upon the four-star product and, as a result, several members of the kitchen brigade, sales team, and other hotel functions moved on, with many leaving during Phil's first month in charge.

He looks back at that period now and describes the staff morale as rock-bottom, with a huge degree of animosity directed at Premier

Inn in general, and himself in particular as Premier Inn's representative. I got the feeling, when hearing him describe the environment pervading throughout the hotel at that time that, had he known what was ahead of him, he would not have taken up the challenge. However, two years on, the situation has certainly changed: the hotel is now operated successfully by a highly motivated staff, led by a committed and professional management team. This transformation, created by Phil, provides us with a classic case study in change management: how to substantially change the direction and operation of an organisation by securing the support of its people. How to persuade them that the changes will benefit them, as well as the company. How to capture their hearts and minds.

Phil decided initially to make very few changes. Indeed, for the first month he spent most of his time wandering around the premises, talking with the staff, hearing what they had to say and beginning the process of building relationships with them. During that time, if he saw practices that he was unhappy with or were counter to the Premier Inn brand, but did not impact negatively on their customers or pose a health and safety risk, he took no action other than to make a mental note. He saw his role during those early days as finding out why things were done the way they were, whilst carefully planting the seeds of change – *"Do you think it might be better for you to ....?"* He was most conscious that the worst thing he could do at that time, as the 'bad guy', would have been to make a raft of early changes.

Phil's strategy was to gradually gain support from individual members of staff through this 'softly-softly' approach. He identified several key members of the team who, if he obtained their buy-in, may act as 'champions of change'. He recognised those people who already provided exceptional service, who had great communication skills and who were positive about the change process. In several cases these key personnel were 'encouraged', and subsequently supported, to take on new challenges and responsibilities. Phil was confident in his belief that development of key personnel would create a positive impression amongst the remainder of the team. Seeing that some colleagues are benefiting from the change process can prove an incentive for others to take tentative steps forward.

However, as is often the case in such situations, some of the staff continued to resist any changes resulting from the hotel's conversion. During the first 12 months, Phil worked hard to explain and embed the Premier Inn philosophy which, for him, is 'to provide a four-star service at a budget price'. Hence he encouraged the hotel team to accept that conversion was a natural extension of the development work they had previously undertaken. In fact, for some departments such as housekeeping the product did not change significantly: their role was still to provide a spotlessly clean room and to help ensure the guests had a great stay.

For others, such as those in the food and beverage departments, things did have to change. A traditional, formal dining service became much more personal; where the serving staff were encouraged to interact with the customers on a less formal, more personal level. For the kitchen staff, the menus became more casual, replacing classical dishes with, albeit well-cooked and presented, more traditional fayre.

At this time, Phil recalled a Whitbread conference he had attended some years previously where the keynote speaker, Sir Clive Woodward, spoke about the corrosive effect of 'energy sappers' – those who would not embrace change and whose attitude had a demotivating influence on others around them. One of Phil's greatest challenges during his first 18 months at the hotel was to face up to, and hopefully convert, those energy sappers. His approach was to hold open and honest one-to-one meetings with them in an attempt to bring their fears, reservations and resentments out into the open. Only by providing opportunities for both sides of the change process to air their views can understanding and compromise be achieved.

Most members of staff, even those most recalcitrant, over time came to realise that their interests would be best served by joining Phil on his journey of change. Most, that is, but not all – despite Phil's best efforts there remained a minority who continued to reflect back to the halcyon days of Golden Tulip and, hence, posed an undue influence on their work colleagues. For them, after every effort had been taken to change their attitudes, a line had to be drawn in the sand and they were released.

Of course, for things to change it was imperative that Phil secured the support of his senior people. He therefore spent a great deal of time and effort during the early months to involve them in identifying what was needed to make the conversion successful and, in particular, to identify energy sappers, even from within their midst! Indeed, Phil cites this as one of his most challenging tasks during the conversion process. Many key members of the hotel's senior team had considerably more experience within the hospitality sector than him and, largely, in a full service environment. For the first three months following Premier Inn's purchase of the hotel the most frequently used phrase by many of the team was, *"In Golden Tulip we never did it that way!"* Whilst proving to be a continual irritant, Phil believed that many of those whose initial actions and words, on the face of it, may have been detrimental to the business and his change management process, had the potential to add a great deal to the new brand and, therefore, were worth special effort.

Phil is an avid reader on management theory and is, in fact, studying for a Masters in Business Administration. He knows that the best way to change people's attitude and behaviour is to encourage them to identify what personal benefits would accrue were they accept and support the inevitable. In the case of those who he believed showed potential he made great efforts to understand their motivations and aspirations, and then encouraged them to accept that they could be furthered by working in partnership with him to effect the necessary changes within the hotel. Many conversations ensued in which career development steps were mapped out, new opportunities identified, and both short- and long-term goals were discussed.

Another of Phil's transformational approaches was to encourage his management team to identify the energy sappers from within their own teams and to reflect on the effect they had on their colleagues, encouraging them to turn the mirror back on themselves.

This 18 month period was certainly the most intense and challenging of Phil's working life – one he readily admits he would not want to repeat! Not only did he have to face up to the resentment felt by the staff, but he had to oversee the change to a completely different set of working practices that were alien to both staff and customers alike. For example, at the time of the acquisition Premiere Inn operated a fixed price model which was in contrast to Golden Tulip's flexible rate strategy. A significant volume of this discounted business was removed on conversion, which had an adverse effect on occupancy. The responsibility to halt this occupancy decline and to recoup a not insignificant amount of inherited site-specific ledger debt fell to Phil. In the event, despite his best efforts, these two issues had a negative impact on the hotel's profit in its first year as a Premier Inn and, as a consequence, impacted on the potential bonus payments for the entire management team, including himself!

Phil found the effect that these inherited debts had on his own financial remuneration to be particularly demotivating. From his perspective, he had been asked to absorb the immense workload occasioned by the hotel's conversion, along with the intense pressures it provided, yet he was not, for no fault of his own, to receive the scale of bonus enjoyed by other company general managers who had not faced the challenges he had.

These were difficult times for Phil and, in retrospect, he regrets allowing the support networks he had built up and benefited from in previous posts to decline. When in Liverpool, for example, he would meet and talk with David Hughes (another contributor to this book) on a regular basis. Perhaps one lesson we should all learn from Phil's experience is not to allow ourselves to become isolated in our work cocoons, irrespective of how frenetic the employment environment is.

However, the pace has now slackened for Phil and the hotel operates as smoothly as others within the company. He admits there are still a couple of staff who occasionally slip back into the Golden Tulip mentality, but he has come to realise that sometimes one has to accept that, with some people, a ninety per cent change of attitude may be as good as it gets.

Personally, I found listening to Phil's story extremely enlightening and a powerful lesson in leadership. I asked him how he would define leadership and he talked about the responsibility of a leader to set the tone and direction for his or her team. Leaders need to be excellent communicators, especially in terms of breaking down business strategies into a language all team members can understand. In particular, every member must understand how they can contribute to the bigger picture by their attitude and performance; for example the hotel receptionist maximising occupancy or the waiter encouraging residents to use the restaurant.

For Phil himself, he is motivated by the impact he can make on both the business and the people who make the business happen. He wants to see his staff rewarded for their efforts and given every opportunity to progress their careers. As for his own career development, he aims to use his experiences over the previous two years as building blocks for progression within the company. His vision is to achieve the grade of Brand Operations Director within the next five years and I, for one, would certainly not bet against him achieving it!

<u>2.9 ELLIOT JARDINE</u>

Franchisee, McDonald's Restaurants

FRANCHISING LEADERSHIP

It takes quite a leap of faith to do what Elliot Jardine did, and a significant amount of investment! Even after spending virtually the entire 17 years of his working life with McDonald's, to then move from the relative safety of being a company employee to the uncertainty of self-employment as a franchisee was a huge gamble. Yes, he came from a family of entrepreneurs and yes, he had worked his way up from trainee manager to Operations Manager for the company's Scottish region – but it was still a gamble that could have had far-reaching and drastic results.

It was in 2004 that he acquired the franchise of his first two McDonald's restaurants, situated in Falkirk. Whilst he was personally confident in both the product and the systems supporting its provision, McDonald's were just emerging from a difficult period; having had to face up to a good deal of negative publicity surrounding healthy eating and environmental issues. Having to remortgage his house and take on a huge loan, together totalling £800,000 of debt, certainly did not result in many good nights' sleep for him during his first year of self-employment. However, since those early days Elliot has taken on another four restaurants and now has a business turning over £9.5m a year and employing over 350 staff.

About two-thirds of McDonald's restaurants are operated by franchisees; typically having around four restaurants each. Being a McDonald's franchisee certainly requires a serious financial commitment, with the 20 year lease costing between £50,000 and £500,000; the average being in the order of £200,000. On top of that, the company requires:

- Monthly rent of 6-18 per cent of sales, according to the size of the restaurant.
- A service fee calculated as 5 per cent of sales.
- Four and a half per cent of sales for marketing support and point-of-sale material.

Not surprisingly, having to cover those initial and subsequent on-going costs focuses a franchisee's mind on profitability, with the emphasis on driving up sales. Elliot describes a franchisee as a half-way house between being an employee and having your own business: you work within an established business model, but continually challenge the parameters of the system in order to maximise sales potential. Franchisees have a determination to develop their business that is greater than an employed manager: in Elliot's case, his house was on the line in the early stages!

He explained to me that, in order to ensure consistent standards of Quality, Service and Cleanliness (QSC being a McDonald's mantra), he must maximise his three principle resources: product, equipment and people.

The product is, to a very large extent, outside of a franchisee's control. Product specifications are set centrally, as are supply chains. The menus must confirm to the standard McDonald's format, and product development is undertaken by specialist teams: if a new type of burger is developed and market tested, every McDonald's restaurant, managed or franchised, must promote and sell it. That said, franchisees can set the prices of their products according to local market conditions and can also undertake bespoke promotions. Elliot works hard, for example, to build close community relationships: being involved in the local football club; sitting on the town centre management committees; and making presentations to the likes of the Rotary Club and youth enterprise groups.

The equipment is purchased under the franchise agreement and is purpose-built for a fast-food operation. It is of the highest quality and has the functionality and reliability required to meet the demands of peak period activity.

So, if franchisees have little control over the product and equipment, the only variable that can be utilised to develop the business is people. Having invested so much in the business they need to capitalise on the added value that highly motivated staff can bring to a hospitality operation. A pleasant member of staff, engaging the children in the dining area whilst the parent goes to the counter to order and collect the food, can make a massive impact on the family's dining experience.

I was interested to hear Elliot's views on what sort of leadership approach a franchisee should take, as opposed to a company-employed restaurant manager. He believes that being self-employed encourages leaders to adopt a more inclusive, family-like approach to their staff, rather than a more formal, corporate style. They are more likely to work harder at building mutually-supportive relationships and using their influence as a direct employer to create a culture of engagement and development.

A good franchisee will spend more time in his or her restaurants, getting to know the staff and continually looking for issues or opportunities that can affect their business. It is important to forge emotional connections with individual staff members, to find out what makes them tick, because you rely on them personally – it is, after all, your customers they are serving!

Indeed, a franchisee can influence working conditions more than a company manager: they can, for example, offer more flexible hours in order to improve an employee's work-life balance. Franchisees tend to be older, wiser and more experienced than managers and are, hence, more likely to adopt a fatherly (or motherly!) mentoring approach. Elliot believes that one of his roles is to develop his people, especially the younger ones, as people, as well as workers. Many start working at McDonald's straight from school, possessing few social skills and little employment experience.

A good leader will create a working environment in which young people can learn basic life skills: turning up for work on time; being proud of their appearance; having an attention to detail; and learning how to work successfully alongside others from different backgrounds and cultures. Elliot is proud that many of his staff have grown and developed whilst working in his restaurants and he has no regrets when they move on to face other challenges – at university, for example.

But not every past employee makes that transition successfully. He told me the story of one of his staff who had worked part-time for eight years whilst studying; his last course being a degree in artificial intelligence at Edinburgh University. He was in his third year, but not really enjoying it so he asked Elliot if he could return to work full-time at the restaurant, as he liked working there so much. Having started as an hourly-paid junior member of staff, he now managers one of the restaurants – a £1.5m business with all the associated responsibilities and challenges.

For Elliot, one of the most difficult skills his managers have to acquire is to develop what he calls 'a sixth sense' about their people; to appreciate what motivates each of them; to get the best work output from them; to understand any underlying personal issues that may affect their relationships with other team members. He is aware of the various motivational theories such as Maslow's Hierarchy of Needs; Hertzberg's Hygiene Factors; and McGregor's X-Y Theory, but his managers operate in a fluid world where customer and staff expectations are continually changing. They must, therefore, seek to get the best out of staff, some of whom expect a greater degree of flexibility in their working arrangements; who want more pay but expect to work less for it. The way to create a win-win solution, where employees benefit personally from working hard for the organisation, is for managers to create a culture within their restaurants that provides a fun, engaging environment in which people believe their potential is being fully realised.

For Elliot's part, he believes his most important role is to develop these skills in each of his managers; giving them the ability and confidence to develop highly motivated, high performing teams. One such skill that Elliot mentioned more than once during our meeting was to be able to take hard disciplinary decisions: to have the confidence, after having sought all alternative courses of action, to sit an employee down and explain why it is necessary for them to part company. No managers like facing such situations but in a business where the franchisee has to be continually seeking ways to drive forward sales, employees who are not pulling their weight or, worse, pose a risk of alienating customers cannot be tolerated.

So Elliot spends a good deal of his time and resources developing his senior team. Franchisees can take advantage of McDonald's training programmes, partly funded through their service fees, but Elliot also draws on his own experiences to encourage his managers to understand the fundamental principles of business. To understand, for example, what drive-through customers are seeking to purchase. Yes, they may buy a Big Mac and fries, but the underlying benefit they require is convenience: being served in the shortest possible time. Hence, it is the managers' responsibility to appreciate this need and to ensure their processes, delivered through their staff, meet it.

During recessionary times, people tend to scale down their expenditure on eating out – opting for less formal dining options, to the benefit of operators providing more casual, less expensive alternatives. Hence, providers like McDonald's are riding the storm successfully and franchisees like Elliot, who apply sound managerial skills and who are visible, inspirational leaders, are reaping the benefits of their initial investments. He certainly did not seem to me to be an entrepreneur who was still having sleepless nights – rather, one who was relishing the role of leading and driving forward a successful business.

2.10 GRAHAM BAKER

Restaurant Manager, Ego Restaurants

A RESTAURANT OPENING SPECIALIST

Graham Baker has become quite an expert in opening new restaurants. The Ego restaurant he manages in Kenilworth is the fourth one he has opened – quite a feat, considering his relatively short career in the hospitality industry.

Although still a young man, Graham has had a good deal of experience of restaurant work, having started working in a Pizza Hut kitchen at the age of 16. It was there that he began to learn about the industry and got the bug for the frenetic activity associated with casual dining operations. Although still far from rising to a managerial position, nonetheless he began to appreciate the operational impact of tight stock control, mystery diners and standardised products; also learning how to work alongside more experienced adult workers, whilst having to be responsible for one's own actions.

As a result of this initial exposure to the hospitality industry, he embarked upon an academic route to management with a Higher National Diploma in Hotel, Catering and Institutional Management, following an Advanced GNVQ in the same discipline. Such qualifications involve periods of work placement and Graham took the opportunity to work in the USA at a resort hotel. Interestingly for me, when interviewing Graham I learnt that, after leaving college, his first job was at The Waterhead Hotel in Ambleside, where I had spent a work placement period during my own HND course – albeit many years before him!

After The Waterhead Hotel, Graham held a number of supervisory positions in other operations before being asked to open a newly-renovated restaurant in Leamington Spa, Warwickshire. The Regent Hotel, built in 1819, had been one of the town's landmarks buildings, but had been allowed to deteriorate until its closure in 1998. However, Graham opened it in 2005 as The Leamington Bar and Grill and worked there for two years before fate took a hand in shaping the direction of his future career.

He was on the High Street in Kenilworth, a few miles from Leamington, when a complete stranger began chatting with him, seeking his views about the town and its inhabitants. That man was James Horler, Executive Chairman of Ego Restaurants, who was planning to open a new restaurant in the town. Adding to this coincidental turn of events, Graham had just applied for another job through a recruitment agency owned by James Horler's wife! James obviously liked what he saw in Graham, went back and checked the CV he had sent his wife, noting I am sure Graham's previous experience in opening new restaurants. What better man to take charge of Ego's newest operation? Hence, Graham was given the opportunity to face the biggest challenge of his career to date.

The Ego handover process is short and sweet: the restaurant is commissioned on a Monday, the snags are resolved over the following two days and, on the Wednesday, the new manager is given the keys and begins to work with the staff. Graham described the process of recruiting new staff for the restaurant as being largely intuitive because, with his experience of the casual dining sector and knowledge of Kenilworth, he knew exactly the staff he was looking for - local people who could relate to the local clientele and also, most importantly, those who had both some experience of life and of the catering industry.

The restaurant opened six months prior to our meeting and, even in those recessionary times, things were going well. Graham's wants it to be recognised as Ego's flagship restaurant, although he recognises he has some way yet to go to achieve that vision. He believes it to be the group's most attractively designed restaurant but, whilst business was certainly building, sales were not yet as high as some of the other operations.

Graham's key performance indicators include targets for sales and expenditure on food, drink and labour, as well as external quality audits. He is well aware that success in meeting these targets depends heavily on the performance of his team of up to 25 staff so he works hard to motivate and inspire them. He believes that all his staff deserve to know how the business is performing so full, transparent financial information relating to current performance against future targets is displayed on the staff notice board. He has also introduced means of incentivising an entrepreneurial spirit within his staff, including rewards for maximising sales opportunities.

It was interesting for me to learn how much freedom Graham has to develop his business. As James Horler explained to me in my later interview with him, (Chapter 2.1), Ego believes in empowering its manager to achieve their targets. It agrees the key performance indicators for each restaurant and then, largely, allows its managers to manage. Take staff communications as an example: there are no set procedures but, in Graham's case, he knows how important open communications are to staff morale so he has instigated managers' meetings every week; shift briefings before every shift; and monthly meetings for all his staff. It is fair to say that Graham recognises and revels in the degree of autonomy afforded by Ego – finding it refreshingly different from other companies he has worked for, where the attitude was more akin to *'these are the rules, don't question them!'*

I was also interested to hear Graham's views on what he believes makes an effective restaurant team leader. For him, it involves demonstrating, through one's personality and attitude, an example for team members to follow. They should be able to look up to someone who they see as honest, fair, transparent and consistent – someone who is professional in all he or she does. Graham believes that leadership requires a balance between working closely with staff to ensure they are combining effectively as a team; whilst also being able to step back in order to see the bigger picture (or 'helicoptering' in Action Centred Leadership terminology). The key to being a good leader, he explains, is knowing when to adopt each approach.

Moreover, Graham recognises that inspirational leadership is especially required within the restaurant industry. He has found that relationships between staff and their managers are generally more relaxed than in the hotel sector. With managers expected to spend more time working with their staff on the restaurant floor, they cannot rely on a hierarchical command structure to impose their influence. Hence, restaurant managers have to use goodwill and persuasion, rather than close control, to achieve the task through their people.

Interestingly, in Graham's experience staff from Eastern Europe, whilst being excellent workers, have found the less formal managerial approach difficult to come to terms with. It took some time, for example, to persuade some of them not to refer to him as Mr Baker! Graham recognises that, whilst UK staff's relationships with their supervisors and managers have changed over recent years, workers from some other countries have yet to recognise that a 21st century leader in the UK has to gain respect based on relationships, rather than on position. This is especially true in an industry like hospitality, where staff are required to work hard and long, often unsocial, hours for minimum financial remuneration. Hospitality leaders must, therefore, use a range of alternative motivational techniques to get the best out of their people. The restaurant sector, in particular, does not offer many high skilled, well paid opportunities, especially for customer-facing staff, hence its leaders must be inspired themselves if they hope to inspire their staff.

So what does inspire Graham, I asked? Just as with his own staff, where he tries to be as flexible as possible with his rotas in order to meet their social and family needs, he, himself, increasingly values a positive work-life balance. Whilst fully recognising that to be successful in the restaurant business you have to live and breathe it, he believes that leaders must increasingly recognise that the concept of unquestionable dedication, to the detriment of all other interests, will not automatically be embraced by all restaurant workers, especially those from within the UK.

The industry offers many opportunities for job satisfaction and advancement but its leaders must work hard to meet the aspirations of each individual member of staff if they are to create high-performing teams providing exceptional customer service and, hence, successful restaurant operations – just as Graham does, himself, to great effect.

2.11 PRITPAL SAGOO

Restaurant Manager,
McDonald's Restaurants

THE McDONALD'S MYTH

You know what they say: if you can't get any other job, go down to McDonald's and flip burgers. All you have to do is learn how to say *"How may I help you?"* It's a dead-end job – the last resort of those struggling in the labour market. There is even the term 'McJob' that is used to describe low-paying, low-skill jobs that offer neither prospect of advancement nor job satisfaction.

But is this negative stereotype representative of reality? How does McDonald's match up to other employers in terms of how it treats its staff? The awards it has received certainly appear to paint a very different picture of a company that was:

- Named 'Best Place to Work in Hospitality' in 2008 by the Caterer and Hotelkeeper Magazine for the past three consecutive years.

- Listed as one of the Times 'Top 50 Companies Where Women Want to Work' for the second year in 2008; and one of its Top 100 Graduate Employers for the ninth consecutive year.

- The first large employer to achieve Investor in People profile status.

It was with these apparently conflicting images in my mind that I went to a McDonald's restaurant in Leicester to meet its manager, Pritpal Sagoo. I approached the counter and was met by a young lady with a beaming smile who asked how she could help me. There was obvious warmth in the welcome – certainly not what one would expect from an automaton, educated in the 'have a nice day' school of customer service! I later learnt that she was a crew trainer called Dimple – one of Pritpal's staff who he had identified as having the people skills necessary to become a role model for other staff. Whilst Dimple went off to find Pritpal, a grey-haired member of staff of late middle-age, hardly the stereotype fast food worker, started chatting pleasantly to me about the weather. Apparently, she was a dining room hostess, again chosen by Pritpal for her natural social skills.

They say that ninety per cent of one's lasting impressions are formed in the first ninety seconds and, in this case, the early perception I got was of a highly motivated team that was obviously benefiting from inspirational leadership – an impression that was later confirmed by my meeting with Pritpal.

Along with ninety per cent of McDonald's restaurant managers, he started as a crew member and worked his way up to become manager of his current restaurant, with leadership responsibility for approaching 100 staff. It is not surprising, therefore, that he is committed to the company and acts as an enthusiastic ambassador for its approach to the development of its people – a far cry, he asserts, from the negative stereotype so often portrayed.

For him, as a McDonald's manager, he delights in seeing people grow and develop; not only in terms of learning new work-based skills, but also gaining life skills. So many new employees, he says, are initially reserved but soon benefit from the family culture he seeks to engender in his team. They learn how to deal with other people, both customers and fellow staff; how to cope with the pressure of peak service times; how to multi-task - and after a while their confidence grows and they become more-rounded individuals.

Pritpal certainly takes great pride in the staff members he has encouraged to develop and grow within his team. He told me the story of Kapil, who started in the restaurant as a reserved, shy 19 year old, straight from college. Yet even at an early stage he was asking questions and demonstrating a sound work ethic. Pritpal identified him as having real potential so created opportunities for him to move through different areas of the kitchen and restaurant: to become a kitchen crew trainer; to take up a supervisory position on the counter; and on to an in-house, six-month management training programme; and finally to complete an external training course in London. Upon Kapil's return, Pritpal continued to work with him to put the management theory into practice and to help him come to terms with his new leadership responsibilities. Now he holds his head up high and commands respect throughout the restaurant staff. For Pritpal, the greatest thrill he gets in his job is seeing people grow: to make a difference to their lives.

He explained to me that the approach to inspiring staff to become ambassadors of his restaurant and his company is based upon two approaches: personal leadership and formal training. In a sense, the training begins even before the crew member actually joins the team as they have to undergo a rigorous recruitment process that commences with an on-line psychometric test to assess suitability, followed by an on-site interview in which the candidates are given a number of service scenarios aimed at evaluating the attitudinal behaviours required of the customer-driven, people-focused restaurant industry. Pritpal estimates that 30-40 per cent of applicants pass the psychometric evaluation and only around 15 per cent successfully complete the whole recruitment process. In fact, on the national stage there are 14 applicants for every crew position – so much for the McJob theory!

Once the employee joins the company, he or she is enrolled onto a training programme so comprehensive that, I would personally suggest, it is amongst the best offered within the hospitality industry. Pritpal claimed that, whilst other employers are cutting back on staff development, McDonald's UK is actually allocating increasing resources, £30m annually, to ensure that its staff are trained to encourage repeat business through the provision of a quality product, produced and served by professional staff. The training path for a new starter involves a number of modules grouped under the headings of 'cleanliness', 'quality' and 'service'; successful completion of which results in the award of gold stars worn on the staff uniforms. Pritpal summarised the overall development approach as 'taking the customer journey to enhance the service experience'.

Indeed, not only has the investment that McDonald's have made into training and development helped it ride out the recession, it has also contributed to the pride its staff have in the company. In the latest, independently conducted, *Your Viewpoint* employee survey 79 per cent say that they feel proud to work at McDonald's, whilst 94 per cent believe the skills they gain would be valuable to other employers.

So, whilst McDonald's certainly has an impressive staff development culture, what about the impact of leadership on the performance and motivation of its staff? I asked Pritpal what he thinks makes a great leader and received a response that could have formed the basis of a text book on leadership theory.

Fundamentally, he believes that the foundation of any successful business is its people. It is therefore a leader's role to identify and fulfil the potential that exists within every person. The leader must continually look for indicators that suggest a person has hidden talents that, with careful nurturing, could be developed – just like Kapil who took an interest in each department he worked in and was continually seeking opportunities to extend his knowledge and skills. The leader should, therefore, create a culture that encourages personal development, in the belief that most people are motivated by achievement. It is the leader's role to create an environment where endeavour is valued and rewarded; where people are respected for the contribution they make to their team and their organisation.

However, for Pritpal, a successful team can only be created if all members are aware of what is expected of them – hence it is the leader's responsibility to explain what he or she expects from each team member and then to create the structures and processes that allow those expectations to be met. Each person is different and so the leader must not adopt a 'one size fits all' approach; rather identifying individual needs and using the authority vested within the leader to ensure that those needs are met. However, leaders must not shirk from taking corrective action if it is merited. A happy workplace is founded upon an appropriate balance of control and reward: if no discipline exists within a team there will be members who coast along. People need to know what is expected of them and that, Pritpal asserts, is one of the most important responsibilities of leadership. If leaders provide an example of openness, honesty and integrity, those will be the foundations upon which they can reasonably expect their followers to behave.

I could hardly have summarised the role of a leader better myself!

I have always believed that the principles of leadership are based upon values and behaviour that everyone can understand and apply successfully. Listening to Pritpal, and experiencing the passion with which he explained his approach to getting the best out of his people, only served to reinforce my belief. Anyone subscribing to the myth of McDonald's being the last resort of anyone seeking rewarding employment should take a trip to Leicester and take a leadership lesson from Pritpal.

2.12 MARTINA DUDASOVA

Head Housekeeper, Malmaison

HYGIENE FACTORS

In several parts of this book I have reported that the UK hospitality industry has benefited greatly from the recent influx of workers from the EU Accession States. Several leaders who employ such migrants have told me of their excellent work ethic and natural customer service skills. It was therefore good to meet with Martina Dudasova, Head Housekeeper from the Birmingham Malmaison Hotel, and to hear her interpretation of any different cultural differences, both being a Slovakian herself and as a manager of many workers originating from Eastern Europe.

Martina studied hotel management for three years in the Czech Republic, one of the two independent states that replaced Czechoslovakia in January 1993 – the other being her native Slovakia. During her training, the tutors stressed the crucial importance of English as the language of the international hospitality, travel and tourism industry so, having gained her degree, she came to England with the express intention of improving her command of the language. Her initial intention was to stay only for a year, but five years later she finds herself enjoying her life in the country and her role with Malmaison – a company she speaks very highly of.

Her initial employment was as a room attendant with Jurys Inns, who have over 30 hotels in cities throughout the UK, Ireland and, indeed, the Czech Republic. However, she felt that her career development opportunities with that company were limited so, two years ago, she successfully applied for the Assistant Head Housekeeper position at Malmaison's Mailbox, Birmingham hotel, being promoted to the head of department post ten months later. The hotel has 189 rooms and Martina leads a team of 38 room attendants, linen room staff and public area cleaners.

I suggested to her that housekeeping staff could be characterised as *The Forgotten Few* – a significant proportion of a hotel's staff complement, but those who are rarely seen by its guests. Indeed, the very nature of their work means that they largely work by themselves, servicing rooms, thus they may not even see their fellow team members for several hours of the working day. The hotel's senior management are likely to know the names of the front of house staff but may rarely come into contact with those working on the accommodation floors. Yet housekeeping staff do have a significant role to play in contributing to levels of guest satisfaction. The presentation of a guest's bedroom, not least its cleanliness, will be a major factor in how he or she evaluates the hotel as a whole and, hence, whether or not it will be considered for return visits.

However, the fact that team members are dispersed throughout the hotel's accommodation and public areas does offer leadership challenges to housekeeping managers. In this respect, Martina makes great efforts to communicate with her staff. Every weekday morning she gets her staff together for a team meeting, which she sees as an ideal environment to feedback guests' comments; be they complimentary or offering opportunities to address issues and improve the service. Also, it is Malmaison's practice for managers to hold monthly 'coffee chats' with all their staff: one-to-one meetings where the employee's performance can be discussed, and celebrated if appropriate.

Malmaison takes its responsibility for staff development very seriously. In October 2004, when its nine properties merged with Hotel Du Vin (eight properties), Robert Cook, CEO, and Sean Wheeler, Head of People, sought solutions to the challenges of merging together two separate workforces without destroying the cultures of the two different brands. They wanted to preserve the two distinctive service offerings, whilst encouraging and facilitating the development and cross-over of talent within both. Their solution was to use the training company learnpurple's Talent Toolbox- a web-based HR performance management and communication tool providing functions such as appraisals, succession planning and training needs analysis. For Malmaison, it estimates resulting HR-related savings of approximately £500,000 per annum, not least by drastically reducing labour turnover to 30%, against an industry average of around double that. For Martina, the toolbox provides her with the framework to discuss and plan the career development of her staff. Indeed, she finds that the opportunity to learn new skills can be a significant motivational factor for her team members.

This was an aspect of her role that I was particularly keen to explore with her; especially in respect of those of her staff coming from the new EU states. Within her team of nearly 40, only seven are British – with the remaining being Eastern European, mainly from Poland. Martina explained that most of the migrant workers come to the UK for the better wages it offers. They usually plan to stay for, perhaps, a couple of years whilst they accumulate sufficient money, before returning home to buy the house or flat they have been saving up for. That said, many, like Martina herself, get used to the better standard of living the UK offers and stay longer than they originally planned. For however long they stay, the money they can earn here is important for them, hence they will always be the first to volunteer for any overtime offered – even proactively asking for extra hours if they feel the opportunity may exist.

But does that desire to work longer actually mean that they work harder than their British co-workers, as other leaders have suggested is the case? Interestingly, Martina would not subscribe to that cultural differentiation. From her experience with Jurys Inns and Malmaison it is a team member's personality, rather than nationality, that determines their work ethic. She recalls that one of her best members of staff is British, whilst she has managed less-than-committed Eastern European workers in the past. She accepts that there are some cultural differences but they do not necessarily impact on work performance.

So is it money that primarily motivates her people, especially those from overseas? She suggested that most people are, indeed, motivated by financial reward – but that stimulus is only effective for a limited period of time. After that, they will soon become demotivated again. If leaders want to encourage and inspire team members on a continuous basis they must apply different incentives. For example, Martina has found that her room attendants enthusiastically embrace opportunities to contribute to the success of their department by making suggestions as to how the service they provide could be improved. Some also relish the chance to broaden their skills by, for example, learning how to write staff rotas or being introduced to financial budgeting. Certainly, morale within her team was enhanced greatly when they came second out of 27 other hotel teams in the recent Malmaison's *'Housekeeping Olympics'* competition.

I asked Martina if she had ever heard of Hertzberg's Hygiene Factors. Whilst she had not, what she had just explained to me, without knowing it, was a direct, practical application of that very theory.

In the late 1950s and 1960s, along with other original thinkers in management theory like Maslow and McGregor, the clinical psychologist Frederick Hertzberg was investigating what motivated people at work. He found that the factors that motivate people are not the opposite of those that dissatisfy them: they are not the opposite sides of the same coin. The factors that demotivate workers are inherent matters such as organisational policy, working conditions, status and pay – which he called Hygiene Factors. Even if you improve aspects of these factors all you do, Hertzberg argued, is reduce people's dissatisfaction. Moreover, they will soon become dissatisfied again and want more improvements in these areas. He argued that if you want to permanently improve workers' satisfaction levels then leaders have to apply what he called Motivational Factors, namely: achievement; job satisfaction; advancement; responsibility; and recognition.

How accurately Martina explained Hertzberg's theory, without being aware of its existence! She recognises the limited impact of increased financial reward on her staff's satisfaction levels – whilst relying more on the five Motivational Factors that Hertzberg identified in order to inspire and enthuse them.

Readers not previously aware of this theory may wonder why its creator used the term Hygiene Factors. Let me explain it in terms of Martina's own employment area. In a hotel, guests <u>expect</u> factors such as cleanliness and other good hygiene practices. Having cleaner carpets and bed linen will not have an impact on guest satisfaction, nor add to the fundamental objective of a hotel, which is to feed and house people. However, poor hygiene practices would certainly negatively affect guests' levels of satisfaction and, in terms of food hygiene, potentially their health and well-being. Hence, Hertzberg's Hygiene Factors form a reasonable expectation of employees, but add little to their increasing motivation. That said, if, for example, pay levels or working conditions were below expectation they would considerably demotivate the staff. Motivational theory explained <u>and</u> practically applied in a hotel setting!

So Martina would certainly subscribe to Hertzberg's thinking and finds that it works in practice within her team. But is she alone in that experience? During the first hour of our Certificate in Team Leadership (Appendix C) we give delegates a list of the eleven hygiene and motivational factors, mixed up into alphabetical order, and ask them to rank them in terms of how motivational they, themselves, find them within their own working environments. Before the actual session on Hertzberg on the second day we have analysed all the responses and are able to provide them with the consolidated group ranking. Without exception, most of the factors that motivate the group as a whole will be Hertzberg's Motivational Factors. They are usually the top five on the group's list – never having been less than five of the top six.

There is a real lesson here for hospitality leaders: if you want to motivate your people, find practical means of enhancing levels of:

- <u>Achievement</u> – contributing to the success of their team and themselves.

- <u>Job Satisfaction</u> – a job that offers variation and challenge.

- <u>Advancement</u> – career <u>and</u> personal development.

- <u>Responsibility</u> – the challenge of additional responsibility.

- <u>Recognition</u> – celebrating their achievement.

Martina has done precisely that and is testimony to the positive effect it can have on a hospitality team.

Appendix A

JOHN ADAIR

John Adair is one of the world's leading authorities on leadership and leadership development. Over a million managers worldwide have taken part in the Action-Centred Leadership programmes he pioneered. He had a colourful early career; serving as a platoon commander in the Scots Guards in Egypt before becoming the only national serviceman to serve in the Arab Legion, where he was adjutant of a Bedouin regiment. After national service he qualified as a deckhand in Hull, working on an arctic trawler in Iceland waters, and then as a hospital orderly in the operating theatre of a hospital.

After being a senior lecturer in military history and adviser in leadership training at the Royal Military Academy Sandhurst, and

Associate Director of The Industrial Society, in 1979 John became the world's first Professor of Leadership Studies when he took up the post at the University of Surrey. He has written over 40 books, translated into many languages; recent titles include *'How to Grow Leaders'*, *'Effective Leadership Development'* and *'The Leadership of Mohammed'*

Between 1981 and 1986 he worked with Sir John Harvey-Jones at ICI, introducing a leadership development strategy that helped to change the loss-making, bureaucratic giant into the first British company to make a billion pounds profit.

He holds the higher degrees of Master of Letters from Oxford University and Doctor of Philosophy from King's College London, and he is also a Fellow of the Royal Historical Society. Recently, the People's Republic of China awarded him the title of Honorary Professor in recognition of his *'outstanding research and contribution in the field of Leadership'*.

In 2009, John was appointed Chair of Leadership Studies at the United Nations System Staff College in Turin.

Appendix B

LEADERSHIP EXCELLENCE IN HOSPITALITY

Professor Adele Ladkin

Bournemouth University

aladkin@bournemouth.ac.uk

Alan Cutler

Hospitality Leadership

alan@hospitalityleadership.com

Professor Nigel Hemmington

Bournemouth University

nrhemmington@bournemouth.ac.uk

ABSTRACT

This paper explores leadership excellence in the hospitality industry. The focus of the research is on successful leaders in hospitality in terms of how they perceive leadership excellence and apply it within their roles. Following an overview of previous research into leadership in the hospitality industry, the paper presents initial findings from a sample of successful leaders within the industry. The findings are discussed in terms of implications for both hospitality organisations and individuals seeking to advance their careers and become effective leaders in the different hospitality sectors.

Key Words: Leadership, Excellence, Hospitality

INTRODUCTION

There is little doubt that leadership is an important issue within hospitality organisations. In an industry dominated by service and experiences, staff play an essential role in the delivery of a high quality product, which is central to competitiveness within the industry. In order to motivate and gain the best performances from employees, the role of effective leaders and managers is crucial. Selecting and developing future leaders is a key survival task for most hospitality organisations (Adams and Waddle, 2002). Set against this background, the purpose of this paper is to explore leadership excellence in the hospitality industry.

The rationale for undertaking this research is first, whilst there is a wealth of research on leadership styles and excellence in the generic management field, there is a need to build on leadership research in the context of the hospitality industry (Tracey and Hinkin, 1996; Arendt & Gregoire, 2005). Second, this research focuses on successful leaders in the hospitality industry in terms of how they perceive leadership excellence and apply it within their roles. This takes the research away from the traditional approaches of exploring leadership excellence in terms of leadership styles, and places the emphasis on perceptions of leadership.

In order to achieve its aims, the paper is organised in the following way. First, a brief introduction to the main research themes in leadership in hospitality is given. This is followed by the methodology for the current research. Finally a discussion of the research findings is given and initial conclusions are drawn. It is important to state at the outset that this work is on-going, and the findings and conclusions presented are taken from the early stages of the research.

LEADERSHIP IN HOSPITALITY

There is much research in the areas of leadership, and a comprehensive review of the literature is beyond the scope of this paper. However, previous research into leadership has developed along a variety of themes. For example, a lack of agreed definitions of leadership and the problems of trying to resolve the controversies has been discussed by Yukl, (1994). Educational developments and the issues behind teaching leadership has also been explored in detail (Scheule and Sneed, 2001; Law and Glover, 2000; Arendt & Gregoire, 2005). Selecting and developing future leaders and the importance of this subject has been discussed by Adams and Waddle, (2002) and Hegarty, (2005). The predictors of leadership has been researched by Brownell (2005), and the importance of trust to leadership success (Simons, 2002), and leadership profiles (Burchell, Gregor and Peterson, 2000) have also received attention. Common to all of the research themes is recognition of the importance of leadership in organisations. The need to understand what makes an effective leader, how leadership skills can be developed and the effectiveness of different leadership styles are all elements central to the success of an organisation.

Leadership research in hospitality has been limited to a small number of studies, most of which have significant methodological limitations, including small samples (Gregor and Peterson 2000) and single company studies (Tracey and Hinkin 1994, Worsford 1995). In terms of leadership and leadership training in hospitality, Saunders (2004) identifies a number of themes from the hospitality literature. These are that leaders need vision, have missions and values, they must be able to inspire and build relationships, and the characteristics of good leaders include integrity, honesty, discipline, passion, perceptiveness and tenacity. Tracey and Hinkin (1996) explored the processes of "transformational leadership" from the employees perspective focusing on key outcome variables including openness of communication, mission clarity, role clarity, leaders' satisfaction and leader effectiveness. This research aims to further an understanding of what constitutes leadership excellence in hospitality from the perspective of the leaders themselves.

METHODOLOGY

The research currently being undertaken and presented in this paper has the support of the Hotel and Catering International Management Association (HCIMA), which as the industry professional body, has recognised the need for further research into leadership in the hospitality industry. The research is on-going, and will take place in three main stages. The first stage began in January 2006 and took the form of a questionnaire based survey to HCIMA Fellows. This questionnaire required them to nominate up to three industry leaders who they believed merit recognition for their leadership excellence and for them also to give reasons for their nomination. Although the Fellows of the HCIMA represent a wide range of different sectors, including hotels, education, contract catering, food service, consultancy, local government, and licensed retailers, the initial responses were dominated by one specific demographic group; males aged 46 and over. In order to widen the sample it was decided, therefore, to include HCIMA Members in the survey. This first stage of the research identified a sample of leaders in the industry, and provided an analysis of what peers feel makes an effective leader.

The second stage of the research was to conduct qualitative in-depth interviews with a sample of the leaders identified through the 'Sunday Times 100 Best Companies to Work For' surveys of 2004, 2005 and 2006, and the Caterer and Hotelkeeper's 'Best Companies to work for in Hospitality' award winners. Twelve of the 'Sunday Times 100 Best Companies to Work For' were identified as hospitality companies and these are shown in Table 1 along with the individual identified for interview. At the time of writing only two of these companies had refused to take part in the study. In addition to this, five hospitality companies won awards in the Caterer and

Hotelkeeper competition and these are shown in Table 2. The first of the interviews took place in January 2006, and they are continuing to take place at the time of writing this paper (April 2006).

TABLE 1

Hospitality Companies from the 'Sunday Times 100 Best Companies to Work For' 2004, 2005, 2006

Name	Organisation
Jonathan Wild, Chairman	Betty's & Taylors
Darroch Crawford, Brand Excellence Director	Premier Travel Inn
Michael Bailey, Chief Executive	Compass Group
David Hamdorff, MD	Ragdale Hall
David Welsh, MD	Ringwood Brewery
Julia Rosamond, HR Director	Nando's Chickenland
Stephen Magorrian, MD	Botanic Inns
Rick Holroyd, Joint MD	Holroyd Howe
Jane Littlewood, Sales & Operations Director	Hayley Conference Centres
Neil Goulden, Chief Executive	Gala Bingo
Declined interview	Catering Alliance (Aramark)
Declined interview	Talacre Beach

TABLE 2

Caterer and Hotelkeeper 'Best Companies to Work For in Hospitality'

Name	Organisation
John Stauss, Regional Vice-President	Four Seasons Hotels
Kate Martin, Managing Partner	The Brookwood Partnership
David Preece, Hotel Services Manager	Nottingham City NHS Trust
Mary McLaughlin, MD	La Tasca Restaurants
Paul Mansi, Operations Director	Radisson Edwardian Hotels

The aim of the interviews was to discover how leaders perceive leadership excellence and how they apply it within their roles. The interviews aimed to ascertain information from the leaders in the following areas;

- their perception of their own role as managers or leaders,
- their interpretation of the difference between management and leadership,
- where their leadership skills were learnt,
- what makes an effective leader,
- the effects of the environment on leadership approaches,
- leadership issues specific to the hospitality industry,
- future changes that require different leadership skills,
- advice for aspiring leaders in the hospitality industry.

The final stage of the study will be to undertake in-depth interviews with the leaders identified through the HCIMA Fellows and Members survey. These interviews will have the same objectives as the first round of interviews and will follow the same format exploring the eight areas identified above. As mentioned earlier, these interviews are on-going and the results presented here represent the initial findings from an analysis of the first tranche of five in-depth interviews.

FINDINGS

The research findings to date are in relation to an analysis of the nominations for leadership excellence, the reasons stated for what makes exceptional leaders, and the qualitative findings from the first series of interviews.

In terms of sample size, for the first stage 82 responses were received from the HCIMA Fellows and Members, resulting in 127 nominations. For stage two, five interviews had taken place at the time of writing. The interview respondents were from the catering, brewery and hotel sectors. The respondents were assured that their comments would not attributed in reports of this research and for this reason they are referred to as respondents 1 – 5 in the findings.

Nominations for Leadership Excellence

From the 82 responses from the HCIMA Fellows, 11 people were identified as excellent leaders with three votes or more. The names of these 11 people and their current organisations are shown in Table 3. These people were included in the sample for the in-depth interviews in stage 3. Six of the 11 received five votes or more and the highest number of votes was eight for Jamie Oliver. Both hotels and restaurants are well represented in the sample, and although only one contract caterer is included this sector was well represented in the nominations as a whole. There was some concern at the outset that the nominations would be dominated by the high profile media celebrities; reflecting media profile rather than leadership, however this has not proved to be the case with only two of the sample being what might be defined as media celebrities (Gordon Ramsey and Jamie Oliver).

Analysis of the nominations reveals some interesting aspects and some limitations of the study. Having asked the HCIMA Fellows and Members to nominate leaders, it is perhaps not surprising that the nominated leaders are almost exclusively UK based. This effectively limits the study to leadership in the UK and has led to proposals for a comparative study with other countries and other cultures at a later date. The large number of nominations (127) is also interesting. At one level it probably reflects the range and diversity of the industry (all sectors were represented, including 4 nominations for leaders in higher education), but it also indicates that there is no consensus on who the pre-eminent industry leaders are.

TABLE 3

Excellent Leaders

Name	Organisation
Gordon Ramsay	Gordon Ramsay Holdings
Alastair Storey	Baxter Storey
Sir Rocco Forte	Rocco Forte Hotels
David Michels	Hilton Group
Bob Cotton	British Hospitality Association
Alan Parker	Whitbread Group
Stephen Carter	St Andrews Bay Golf Resort
Peter Taylor	Town House Hotels, Edinburgh
Jamie Oliver	Fifteen
Garry Hawkes	EDGE
Peter Lederer	Gleneagles Hotel

It should also be noted that only 10 of the nominated leaders were female and that none of these received sufficient nominations to be included in the in-depth interviews for this phase of the study. This probably reflects the gender demographics of the industry but may also be the result of the fact that most of the survey respondents were males over the age of 45 (which also reflects the gender balance of the industry). Despite this industry imbalance, it might be interesting to explore gender based dimensions of leadership by extending the study to include a larger sample of female leaders at a later date (4 women leaders were included through the 'best companies to work for' element of the study but this still represents a very small sample).

What makes people exceptional leaders?

The respondents were asked to state up to three reasons why they had nominated the people as exceptional leaders. The results of the analysis of this data are presented in rank order in Table 4.

These findings demonstrate that the most cited reason for leadership excellence is that of being supportive, trusting and looking after staff. Ranked second and fifth is the theme of passion for both the industry and for providing excellence in the industry. The nominated leaders are also influential people who had a positive public profile which they had used to benefit the industry. The ability to motivate people and to make innovative business decisions is also cited as something central to excellence in leadership.

In-depth interviews with leaders

The qualitative data from the five in-depth interviews conducted to date was analysed with regard to the following issues; their perception of their own role as managers or leaders, and the difference between these two terms, where their leadership skills were learnt, what makes an effective leader, the influence of the environment on leadership approaches, leadership issues specific to the hospitality industry, future changes that require different leadership skills, and finally advice for aspiring leaders in the hospitality industry.

1. Perception of own role as managers or leaders and difference between leadership and management. From the five respondents, three saw themselves clearly as leaders, one more as a manager, and one wasn't sure. All agreed that being a manager or a leader was difficult to define, and that being good at both roles was beneficial to the success of the business. There was also an agreement that leadership is more about inspiring, facilitating and empowering, and management was more concerned with the day to day organisation of the business including planning and resources. Comments from the respondents on their leadership roles included:

Table 4

What makes an exceptional leader in the hospitality industry?

Attribute	Number of times mentioned
1. Support/trust/empowerment for staff – doesn't let you sink/strong staff welfare/brings out the best	20
2. Passion for excellence/quality of food/product/service	14
3. Public profile/ability to influence the industry/ambassador	14

4. Build self–belief/inspirational	13
5. Passion for the industry/business	9
6. Makes people want to work for them/motivates/develops teams/team player/infectious work ethic	9
7. Can turn around/refocus companies	9
8. Visionary	8
9. Innovative	6
10. Entrepreneurial	6
11. Strong personality/dynamic/charismatic/good way with people	6
12. Leads from the front/by example/strategic leadership	6
13. Treats everyone fairly and as equals	5
14. Personal approach to service in the industry/values customers	5
15. Commitment to training/education/career development/internal staff development	4

16. Being wise/a thinker	4
17. Generous with time	4
18. Good communication skills – internal and external to industry	3
19. Say what they think/not afraid to stand up for beliefs	3
20. Decent and likable/respected	3
21. Self belief	2
22. Having integrity	2
23. Gets the job done	2

"Managing is more about directing staff to get an agreed outcome, leadership is about involvement, empowerment and facilitation of others to achieve a goal. Leadership takes more confidence, and is often longer term. Management takes more basic skills." (Respondent 1)

"Leaders rise above day to day stuff and don't spend lots of time measuring and monitoring managing. They just excite people and are open to new ideas. They should be open to new ideas and not be afraid to get their hands dirty. They should inspire." (Respondent 2).

"Good management and good businesses tend to be run by good leaders, not managers. Management can be destructive. You need the management skills though to be a successful leader." (Respondent 3).

"Leaders are more a figurehead, leading by example and having a strong personality. Managers facilitate how the get the best out of the business." (Respondent 4).

"Managing is more organisational. Leadership is a gift and a privilege. You have to build trust." (Respondent 5).

2. Where leadership skills were learnt. The respondents had learnt their leadership skills from a range of different sources. Common to all respondents was that they had learnt from other people, and three respondents stated this was from people who were both good and bad. There were also comments relating to learning by trial and error, and being given sound advice by one or more people. None of the respondents mentioned they were 'born' leaders, but had listened and learnt from others.

3. What makes an effective leader? The respondents commented on two main issues that are seen as crucial in being an effective leader. The first is the importance of communication, and the second is in relation to staff. This is to be supportive of staff, to give people credit and trust, and to try and make people feel valued. An effective leader is someone who

"is a good communicator devotes lots of time to staff, is supportive, is a good role model, and practices what they preach" (Respondent 1).

They should have:

"Enthusiasm and a sense of humour, be a good listener and give credit. Have trust in staff and be prepared to admit mistakes" (Respondent 2).

The respondents discussed ways in which communication could take place, whether this is in the form of monthly meetings, bulletins, discussions with line managers etc, and communication should not always be just top down. The key idea behind communication as a crucial element of effective leadership is that keeping people informed makes people feel part of the organisation and good communication is essential for businesses to be successful. Empowering staff and making them feel valued is also beneficial to businesses both in terms of their success and creating positive work environments.

4. The influence of the environment on leadership approaches. The respondents had mixed views on whether the working environment does have an influence on leadership approaches. One comment was that the leadership approach depends on the current development and status of the team they are working with. For example, leadership will change over time between setting up a new team of people to work together as opposed to groups who have worked together for a long time. Another respondent commented that the size of the business could also have an influence; it takes a different leadership approach in working with a small business, where the leader has regular contact with all staff, as opposed to those who are leading large fragmented organisations. Other comments were that good leaders do not change their approach as they are always 'credible'. One respondent raised the issue that business environments fluctuate between times of success and times of difficulty, and reported that leaders;

"Have to be able to lead in both good and bad times." (Respondent 5).

5. Leadership issues specific to the hospitality industry. Each of the respondents felt there were particular characteristics of the hospitality industry that created specific issues for leaders. A key factor was the importance of looking after staff as they are crucial to the success of the business. This was summarised by one of the respondents as:

> *"Look after your staff. Take care of your staff and they will take care of the customers"* (Respondent 5).

There were also issues raised in relation to the nature and characteristics of the hospitality industry. Comments included:

> *"The catering sector does not have a good reputation for leadership: it is very authoritarian, bureaucratic and macho. It has stifled development of the industry as it puts people off. Low pay and high turnover of staff can make developing relationships difficult, which makes looking after staff very important."* (Respondent 1).

The competitive environment in the hospitality industry was also seen to have an influence on leadership. One comment was

> *"It is a competitive environment at the moment, so you have to engender brand loyalty"* (Respondent 3).

6. Future challenges that require different leadership skills. Similar issues to those raised above were discussed by respondents in relation to future challenges that may affect leadership in the industry. The issues raised were quality of staff, mobile and transient labour, consolidation and competition. The following quotes illustrate these issues;

"There is a struggle for quality staff in transient labour markets and competition for labour between companies. Leaders will have to look after staff well." (Respondent 1).

"There is more consolidation in the industry. Businesses are getting larger and national brands more common. The challenge is whether you can have the same influence and leadership in a large organisation." (Respondent 3).

Further comments were made regarding the multi-cultural workforce characteristics in many hospitality sectors.

"When bringing in staff from non-hospitality backgrounds, you can lean new things from them". (Respondent 3).

"There are cultural and language issues". (Respondent 5).

7. Advice for aspiring leaders in the hospitality industry. Each of the respondents had advice for those aspiring to be leaders in the hospitality industry. The comments tended to focus on honesty, integrity and openness, and included comments such as:

"Have the self confidence to involve your team in decision making". (Respondent 1).

"Be honest in your approach. Have a transparent approach in dealing with one's staff". (Respondent 2)

"Be yourself – be honest and do what you say you will do." (Respondent 3).

"Listen and learn – don't feel you have to stamp your authority from the first day. Be honest about your strengths and weaknesses, and share them. Work with a team". (Respondent 4)

"If you don't believe in the cause after time, leave it." (Respondent 5)

The need to recognise personal strengths and weaknesses and having the confidence to share these with the team is an interesting dimension. The notion of confidence and teamwork is also recognised in the comment about involving the team in decision making. These comments perhaps signal a move away from the all powerful, 'great man' view of leadership in hospitality towards an approach based on facilitation through teams of experts.

CONCLUSIONS

Despite the research being in its early stages, initial findings have implications for both hospitality organisations and individuals seeking to become excellent leaders in the hospitality industry.

In terms of organisations, both the comments from the HCIMA Fellows and Members on what people felt were essential attributes for leadership excellence and the interview respondents, they felt that looking after and supporting staff, engendering trust, and making staff feel valued is vital. This is seen as crucial for the success of the business as contented and motivated staff provide a better service; a good working environment makes things better for everyone. The interview respondents indicated that communication is central to running an effective business and to keep staff motivated and to feel part of a team. The importance of trust to leadership success echoes previous research by Simons (2002), and open communication is advocated by Tracey and Hinkin (1994). The idea behind both of these issues that if people work together and feel valued it is good for business success and makes working life more enjoyable. Organisations should also consider the influence of a transient workforce, where staff turnover is high particularly in the unskilled jobs. In order to recruit and retain quality staff, a positive working environment is essential.

With regard to individuals, the findings from the attributes required for leadership excellence and the interview respondents revealed a number of common themes. These include leading by example, being prepared to pull weight in all areas when required, to be honest and have integrity, to admit weaknesses, learn from mistakes, and have a passion for excellence. Most importantly is the need to be enthusiastic and passionate about your chosen industry, and to look after staff well. Future leaders should be prepared to listen and learn from others as they develop their careers.

Perhaps the most significant finding of the research to date is that although those interviewed thought that there were particular characteristics of the hospitality industry that create specific issues for leaders, none of the issues identified were peculiar to the hospitality industry. Indeed, the identified characteristics of effective leaders were all generic management and leadership skills. Furthermore, the advice for aspiring hospitality leaders was generic and could apply to leadership in any industry. It is too early in the research to conclude that hospitality leadership is no different from leadership in other sectors but this is clearly an area that needs further exploration and analysis in the later stages of the research.

It is anticipated that the on-going research presented here will add to these findings and that this research will identify areas for further research. As mentioned earlier, comparative research in at least one other country is already planned. Research that includes a significant sample of women leaders may also raise some interesting additional dimensions and facilitate cross-gender analysis.

REFERENCES

Arendt, S.W. and Gregoire, M.B. (2005), Leadership behaviours in hospitality management students, *Journal of Hospitality & Tourism Education,* 17(4): 20-27.

Adams, D., and Waddle, C. (2002). Evaluating the return from management development programmes: individual returns versus organisational benefits. *Journal of Contemporary Hospitality Management,* 14(1):14-21.

Brownell, J. (2005). Predicting leadership: The assessment centre's role. *International Journal of Contemporary Hospitality Management,* 17(1): 7-21.

Burchell, J., Gregor, K.R., and Peterson, J.S. (2000). leadership profiles for the new millennium. *Cornell Hotel and Restaurant Administration quarterly,* 41(1): 16-29.

Hegarty, J., (2005). *Leadership for change in hospitality and tourism education.* The 23rd EuroCHRIE Conference 'Facing change in tourism and hospitality', October 26-28 2005, Paris, France.

Law, S., and Glover, D. (2000). *Educational leadership and learning: practice, policy and research.* Buckingham, Open University Press.

Saunders, R.E. (2004). Leadership training in hospitality. *Florida International University Hospitality Review,* 22(1): 30-40.

Scheule, B., and Sneed, J. (2001). Teaching leadership in hospitality management programmes: A model for learning from leaders. *Journal of Hospitality and Tourism Education,* 13(2): 34-37.

Simmons, T. (2002). The high cost of lost trust. *Harvard Business Review,* 80(9): 18-21.

Tracey, J.B. and Hinkin, T.R. (1994), Transformational leaders in the hospitality industry, *Cornell Hotel and Restaurant Quarterly,* 35(2): 18-24.

Tracey, J.B. and Hinkin, T.R. (1996), How transformational leaders lead in the hospitality industry, *International Journal of Hospitality Management,* 15(2): 165-176.

Worsfold, P. (1995), Leadership and managerial effectiveness in the hospitality industry, *International Journal of Hospitality Management,* .8(2):145-155.

Yukl, G. (1994). *Leadership in Organisations.* 3rd edition, Englewood Cliffs NJ, Prentice Hall.

ADDITIONAL FINDINGS RESULTING FROM FURTHER RESEARCH (2007)

Further research focused on three industry-specific themes that were raised during the survey undertaken in 2006. Selected telephone interviews were held with a number of the hospitality leaders involved in the initial research to seek their views of questions relating to the three themes, as follows:

THEME A - INCREASING CUSTOMER EXPECTATIONS

Is this the case? There was an overwhelming view that customer expectations were increasing across the industry and this was seen as a positive thing. Customers have higher expectations and are much more 'tuned in' to what they can expect. Increasing competition in the sector has driven quality standards upwards and people have got used to expecting more.

What can leaders do to encourage their staff to give exceptional customer service? Many practical examples of what can be done were identified by the interviewees, including training, constant communications, making people aware of what is expected etc. The overall message was one of culture - creating a working environment and organisational culture that is supportive of people, treats them fairly and encourages them to provide the best possible service. It was a case of making the organisation a good place to work in.

Does recruitment play a part? All respondents stressed having an appropriate recruitment strategy as being crucial - one based on hiring personality and attitude and then training skills and knowledge once the person is employed.

THEME B - THE PROFILE OF INDUSTRY STAFF

Is an increasing proportion of hospitality staff multi-cultural and transient? All the respondents agreed that the profile of hospitality workers is, indeed, changing (especially with regard to there being more workers from Eastern Europe), although it was more the case in the hotel and restaurant sector than with contract catering. Many interviewees made the point that this is not necessarily a new phenomenon as other nationalities, such as Philippines and Portuguese, have always worked in the sector. The change over recent years is that the numbers of 'migrant' workers have increased and more are from the new EU states. There was agreement that this trend is a very positive thing, with many of the leaders stating that they could not operate without these workers. In particular, Polish workers were found to have an excellent work ethic and attitude.

What are the implications for hospitality leaders? Issues raised for leaders who have to manage a multi-cultural workforce included: giving appropriate training; encouraging language training; treating people as equals; and having cultural sensitivity.

THEME C - THE INDUSTRY'S REPUTATION

Does the reputation of the hospitality industry put people off joining it? The view was that the industry was still perceived to be (and, in some cases, still is) a poor working environment with bad conditions of employment, although the respondents felt that this was changing. This perception should be challenged by organisations making sure that their workplaces were rewarding to work in.

How can hospitality leaders influence their industry's reputation? Leaders should lead by example by ensuring that they not only provided fulfilling jobs, but should also go out of their way to promote the industry. They should work with industry bodies and consider entering initiatives such as The Sunday Times '100 Best Companies to Work For' survey. There was also a strong feeling that leaders could work with schools, career advisors and parents to explain the myths and realities of the industry, and to stress its potential benefits such as excellent career development opportunities and the potential to work overseas.

Appendix C

INSPIRATIONAL TEAM LEADERSHIP

An inspirational two-day training programme based upon John Adair's Action Centred Leadership model, accredited by The Confederation of Tourism and Hospitality and delivered by trainers approved by Hospitality Leadership Ltd.

'Aspire to Inspire'

Hospitality Leadership

Who Should Attend:

Employees who either currently lead teams within service organisations, such as supervisors or junior managers, or are seen as having the potential to take up team leadership roles.

Course Outcomes:

At the end of the course, trainees will be able to:

- Understand what is meant by leadership and the role of a team leader.

- Understand and apply the principles of Action Centred Leadership (ACL) within a workplace.
- Draw up a plan of action to improve their leadership skills according to the principles of ACL.

Benefits for Organisations:

Team leaders who understand and apply effective leadership skills and:

- Lead more highly motivated teams.
- Have higher levels of transferable leadership skills.
- Have the foundation of leadership skills upon which they can develop into operational leadership roles.
- Whose teams provide improved standards of customer service.
- Who lead teams that contribute positively to their organisation's image and competitiveness.
- Whose teams enjoy lower levels of staff turnover.

Course Overview:

This is a unique development course focusing entirely on the team leadership qualities required in service-driven industries. It is based upon John Adair's ACL, which is represented by three overlapping circles that denote a leader's main responsibilities to:

➢ Achieve the **task**
➢ Build and maintain the **team**
➢ Develop the **individual**

However, not only is it highly **relevant** to those leading service teams, it is also:

Practical – an opportunity to 'learn by doing'.

Participative – every trainee will have at least one opportunity to lead a team through an exercise, one opportunity to observe the leadership of an exercise and numerous opportunities to experience and review the leadership of other trainees.

Varied – using a range of learning methods.

Action-oriented – trainees draw up a plan of specific actions and commit themselves to addressing them upon return to their work.

Challenging – trainees are encouraged to face up to the demands of their roles.

Enjoyable – people learn best when they are enjoying themselves – and they will on this course!

Accreditation:

Certificates will be awarded for successful completion of a 45 minute, externally marked, assessment of learning, based upon a given ACL case study. It can be taken as an extension to the end of the course, or at a later time, according to the wishes of the client.

Comments from some past trainees:

"The leadership exercises forced me out of my comfort zone."

"I loved to see others change and improve, and smile about it."

"I was not expecting it to be so informative and fun."

"It was one of the best seminars I have ever attended."

"The leadership exercises were brilliant to put the principles into practice, and the in-depth feedback at an impersonal level worked really well."

What Jasminder Singh, Chairman of Radisson Edwardian Hotels, said after the training was included in his company's 'Future Leaders' programme:

"I am pleased to confirm that, having considered the content, delivery and assessment of The Inspirational Team Leadership training programme, I fully recognise its ability to develop the future managers and leaders of the hotel industry.

Initiatives to increase the skill levels and knowledge of both new entrants and existing managers within the industry are welcomed by Radisson Edwardian Hotels. I believe that this course provides a valuable foundation for those who have an interest in pursuing a successful management career in the international hospitality industry"

And a final word from John Adair himself:

"The hospitality industry, being so people-centred and customer-focused, needs inspirational leadership in all its sectors. I am pleased, therefore, to be able to support the work that my Associate, Alan Cutler from Hospitality Leadership Ltd, is doing to raise standards of leadership throughout his industry. I believe that Alan and his colleagues have a real contribution to make at every level of leadership."

Please contact inspire@hospitalityleadership.com for more information about the course

Appendix D

MANAGEMENT SKILLS CHECKLIST

(To be used in conjunction with a Training Needs Analysis, as described on page 100, Chapter 1.5)

Motivation

1. Encouraging my team members to take a real interest in their jobs

2. Generating great morale within my team

3. Motivating an individual who has the ability, but does not apply it

4. Persuading my team to see what has to be done, and to do it without being told

Teamwork

5. Helping team members to work together effectively

6. Dealing with personality clashes within the team

7. Dealing with individuals who do not take their fair share of the workload

8. Developing productive working relations between my team and others

Delegation

9. Knowing the jobs only I can undertake and being prepared to ask others to do some of my other work

10. Dealing with individuals who are keen to take on more responsibility that I know they cannot handle

11. Dealing with individuals who could take on more responsibility, but do not want to

Dealing with problems

12. Choosing the best of several alternative ways of doing a job

13. Identifying the real problem in a difficult situation

14. Organising a complicated problem into manageable tasks

15. Dealing with difficult staff issues in the early stages

Training

16. Undertaking induction training promptly and effectively

17. Assessing whether my team members know how to do their jobs

18. Measuring the effectiveness of the training my team receives

19. Training my team members on-the-job

Performance

20. Setting achievable standards for myself and others

21. Evaluating my own and others' performance fairly

22. Correcting poor performance promptly and effectively

23. Helping others who have personal problems that affect their job performance

Planning

24. Planning the work of my team in the most efficient manner

25. Monitoring work progress against the plan

26. Anticipating problems that might block the work's progress

27. Prioritising tasks against external requirements

28. Using the resources of my team effectively by allocating work appropriate to individuals' strengths and weaknesses

Time

29. Dealing with excessive demands placed upon my time by other people

30. Using my time effectively each day

Ideas

31. Generating suggestions from my team

32. Encouraging my team to accept new ways of doing things

33. Selling new ideas to my manager

Communications

34. Explaining clearly what I expect from my team

35. Creating effective communications with my manager

36. Running productive meetings with others

37. Passing down information to my staff that I have received from others

38. Being able to make persuasive presentations to key decision-makers

Customer-related skills (to be adapted for individual working environment)

39. Producing and/or serving food of a quality my customers require

40. Presenting the food within service areas in a way to maximise profit potential

41. Identifying customer expectations

42. Providing a flexible service to all customer groups

43. Building productive, supportive relations with my client(s)

44. Dealing with difficult managers within my client's organisation

Financial skills (to be adapted for individual working environment)

45. Understanding budgets

46. Monitoring performance by means of food cost percentages

47. Monitoring performance by means of labour cost percentages

48. Identifying and taking sales opportunities in order to maximise income generation

49. Being able to justify operating costs to interested parties

Specialist skills (to be adapted for individual working environment)

50. Taking a responsible approach to the requirements of food safety legislation

51. Promoting environmental policies

52. Making the most of available IT resources

53. Undertaking all written work, including bookkeeping, accurately and legibly

54. Completing all bookwork and returns required of me by the due date

Appendix E

PEARLS OF WISDOM

The $64,000 Question

"If you had to give one piece of advice to someone entering the hospitality industry as a leader with similar responsibilities as yourself, what would it be?"

2.1 James Horler, Chief Executive, Ego Restaurants

"In the restaurant industry, you only get out what you put in. There is no other industry that rewards hard work so well"

2.2 John Stauss, Regional Vice President, Four Seasons Hotels

"Be open-minded, adaptable and flexible. Be prepared to think like a guest; think like a member of staff; adapt to economic cycles and the ever-changing world of work. Having the ability to ride on the wave, on its peaks and troughs, will become more and more important to our industry"

2.3 Stuart Bowery, Cluster General Manager, Marriott Hotels

"Have a clear moral compass: display humility, compassion and empathy but be absolutely clear on what you will not compromise on. You will only get what you expect – if you are prepared to compromise, that is what you will get"

2.4 Graham Olds, Operations Director, Holroyd Howe Independent

"Whatever task you are given, undertake it to the best of your ability. Before you deliver it, ask yourself and others if it will meet the highest possible standards"

2.5 Gary Dodds, Regional Vice President of Human Resources, Marriott Hotels

"You have to have a passion for leading people in providing a service to others. If you are not comfortable with the concept of serving people with a sense of pride, not servitude, you are in the wrong business"

2.6 Stephen Philips, Operations Manager, Brookwood Partnership

"Never seek to hide from your mistakes because you can be sure that, in the future, one of them will return to bite you. Show me a person who has never made a mistake and I will show you someone who has never achieved anything"

2.7 David Hughes, General Manager, Premier Inn

"Accept the responsibility of your position. Act as an umbrella – if the team is successful put the umbrella down and celebrate in their success. However, if a problem arises open the umbrella above the team to protect them from both the cause and effect of the problem"

2.8 Phil Scott, General Manager, Premier Inn

"When faced with a management situation, never underestimate the importance of communications at every level in order to ensure that each team member understands what needs to be achieved and how they can make a personal contribution"

2.9 Elliot Jardine, Franchisee, McDonald's Restaurants

"Leadership can be a lonely place, so have someone alongside you, acting as a sounding board, to ensure you are going in the right direction. Adopt a healthy paranoia: do not be complacent and constantly review progress in terms of both your business and your people"

2.10 Graham Baker, Restaurant Manager, Ego Restaurants

"Be prepared to accept that the restaurant industry will place heavy demands upon your life. You can have a satisfactory work-life balance, but be prepared to be flexible, adaptable and accept the hours and shift patterns required of a restaurant team leader"

2.11 Pritpal Sagoo, Manager, McDonald's Restaurants

"Be confident in your own ability to achieve your objectives; be open-minded to change; and be humble enough to learn from those around you

2.12 Martina Dudasova, Head Housekeeper, Malmaison

"You must enjoy yourself. If not, what is the point? Be passionate about your job and reap the rewards that the hospitality industry offers to those who go the extra mile."

INDEX